C000181079

THE AUTOBIOGRAPHY OF AN
EXMOOR POACHER

EDITED BY
"CARACTACUS"

*"He did not know that a gamekeeper is only
a poacher turned outside in, and a poacher
a gamekeeper turned inside out."*
KINGSLEY, *Water Babies*

First published by John Macqueen 1901
Second facsimile edition 2002

ISBN 1 84114 158 5

British Library Cataloguing-in-Publication Data
A CIP record for this title is available from the British Library

HALSGROVE
Halsgrove House
Lower Moor Way
Tiverton, Devon EX16 6SS
T: 01884 243242
F: 01884 243325
sales@halsgrove.com
www.halsgrove.com

Printed and bound in Great Britain by
Bookcraft Ltd, Midsomer Norton

PREFACE

POACHERS, like pirates, and, indeed, all without the pale of civilisation and convention, are interesting folk; and Holcombe, the hero of his own story, freely recognises the fact. Possessing a fund of anecdote, he has covenanted to atone for all the trouble he once caused by relating to a younger generation his parti-coloured experiences. Though not a practised writer, he is a great reader, especially of newspapers, and he stipulated that his adventures should be set forth, not in the West Somerset dialect, which he occasionally affects, but in good, sound, proper newspaper English, that can be read with comfort in Great Britain and Ireland, the Colonies, and even the United States of America. With this sensible request, his amanuensis and friend has done his best to comply, but he has not for that reason deemed it necessary to weed out every provincial term or provincial phrase; and, throughout, he has

PREFACE

been careful to preserve the turn of thought, always more important than the precise words in which the thought has been expressed.

Holcombe's deer - killing proclivities link him with famous Robin Hood, perhaps in his day as great a nuisance to keepers; and in a Dulverton ditty, "old Robin Hood, the forester bold," is yet renowned. The immortal Shakespeare, according to tradition, was in youth a deer-stealer; and Gilbert White in his "History of Selborne," observes that "most men are sportsmen by constitution, and there is such an inherent spirit for hunting in human nature as scarce any inhibitions can restrain." Afterwards, to show his intimacy with the irregular contingent, he goes on:

"Our old race of deer-stealers are hardly extinct yet; it was but a little while ago that they used to recount, over their ale, the exploits of their youth; such as watching the pregnant hind to her lair, and when the calf was dropped, paring its feet with a pen-knife to the quick to prevent its escape, till it was large enough and fat enough to be killed; the shooting at one of their neighbours with a bullet in the turnip-field by moonshine, mistaking him for a deer; and the losing a dog in the following

PREFACE

extraordinary manner:—Some fellows suspecting that a calf new-fallen was deposited in a certain spot of thick fern, went with a lurcher to surprise it; when the parent hind rushed out of the brake, and, taking a vast spring with all her feet together, pitched upon the neck of the dog and broke it short in two." Holcombe, too, has had a rare experience with a hind, having been present at the accouchement of one, a thing, he opines, of which no other living man can truthfully boast.

Scrope's "Art of Deer-stalking" contains sundry anecdotes of poachers and freebooters in bonnie Scotland, and Richard Jefferies, in his "Red Deer," relates a fine story about an Exmoor poacher. The last-named authority dwells on the revolution in local ideas as to the legitimacy of the practice.

Formerly, "if anyone sighted a stag, or found the slot, he roused the country-side; people armed themselves with guns of every kind and sallied forth to destroy it. If a stag was shot, he was put into a cart, and carried through the place in triumph."

Now, "were a man to shoot a stag he would be utterly sent to Coventry. No one would speak or deal with him, or acknowledge his

b

PREFACE

existence. He would be utterly cut off from society of every class, not only the upper but the lower classes being equally imbued with the sporting spirit."

Written nearly twenty years ago, these words are not less true to-day. Deer-poaching, in fact, is as extinct as wrecking, and, with the spirit that animates the Exmoor people, certain never to be revived. This certainty invests with exceptional interest the following narrative, which rescues from oblivion an almost forgotten phase of West Country life. Holcombe's poaching exploits were, however, general as well as particular, and he has also contributed a sketch of his compromise with civilisation during the time he masked his real self under the guise of a keeper.

It only remains to add that "his lordship" is no figment, but lives in Dulverton, where, at the conclusion of the performance, he will metaphorically, and very delicately, pass round the hat.

"CARACTACUS."

CONTENTS

THE AUTOBIOGRAPHY OF A POACHER

CHAPTER I

HOW I WENT ON WHEN I WAS A BOY

I WAS born and bred at Dulverton, a fact of which I am proud. It is one of the best places for sport in the West of England ; and, as I have travelled in other parts, I can testify one of the prettiest. But I suppose everybody is inclined to favour the spot where he spent his youth, and, maybe, great part of his manhood, so I will not dwell long on that. I will merely observe that the town lies in the heart of beautiful sloping woodlands, through which come tumbling Barle and Exe, twin - rivers, from the heights of Exmoor. These streams abound in fish, not so much perhaps as in my young days, but on that subject I shall have a good deal to say presently.

Now it is a curious thing that, although I lodge in a very nice cottage at the higher end of the town, I never feel entirely at home there. Possibly, the air is cold. Anyhow, I was brought up in a more sheltered quarter. My father lived in a low-lying street, just off the Little Bridge, and known in those days as Duck Paddle. Clever artists reside at Dulverton, and others stay here, from time to time, as visitors; I reckon they would consider our cottage picturesque. It was old-fashioned, had a thatch roof, and, to enter, you had to go down a step. Across the kitchen ceiling ran a thick beam, black with smoke, and nailed to the beam were slots, one for each deer we killed.

As I grew up I took a great pride in those feet, which I helped to multiply. I cleaned and brushed them and oiled them about the hoofs. I may add that, in later times, others besides myself took an interest in the slots. There was then at Dulverton a silk factory, the fabric of which still remains, and now serves as a laundry. In this factory were employed a fine lot of girls, seventy or eighty in number, and of all countries, and amongst them I had a fancy maiden or two. When I killed a deer, I used to celebrate the event by treating them. During the dinner-hour I would take half-a-dozen of the girls and three or four chaps to one of the public-houses in the town, and give them a quart of egg-flip, which was meat and drink both. You will understand, therefore, that the pretty things often peeped in to see if there were any addition to the slots, hoping for more egg-flip.

Our next door neighbour was a noted character called " Ned the Sweep." On fair-days he was hired to stand outside the booths, and offer to box. You paid twopence to go in, and, as boxing was popular, the booths were generally full, some with the gloves on, and others watching. Father was a shoemaker by occupation, but, like a good many others, eked out a living by poaching. As I grew up, I helped him occasionally at his trade, but I was never a proper shoemaker.

One of my earliest recollections concerns Barle river. The gentlemen had it staked to prevent a certain kind of fishing—that is, with drag nets. Well, the fishermen of Dulverton, about a dozen in number, amongst whom was my father, agreed together to go down with axes and bars of iron, and saw off or pull up the stakes, wherever they found them. The bridge

3

was crowded with spectators, including the gentlemen that ordered the work to be done; and, as the men threw the stakes out of the river, the old women carried them off to burn them. The consequence was that the criminals were had up before the justices sitting at the Red Lion, and committed to Taunton Jail for trial. However, the Dulverton people made a collection and sent for a lawyer of Exeter, called Furlong. This gentleman procured the fishermen's release, and home they came, marching through the streets with flags and singing a song, which, as nearly as I can recollect, was as follows :—

> We are all out of jail,
> And homewards we are steering;
> And now we do return again,
> We'll fish the Barle ten times more.
> That's good luck, so says I,
> Right for the diddle-o-the-dido.

When I was young, my father used to go to the stag-huntings, and the rule was that when the deer was run up and in the water, the man who first seized him by the horns received a crown. He had also the privilege of carrying round the head, first perhaps to Pixton, if anybody was at home, and afterwards to Baron's

HOW I WENT ON WHEN A BOY

Down, Hollam, Combe, all great houses in our neighbourhood. Then he would back and show it to the gentry living in the town, and at all the public-houses, where he would put a horn in the deer's mouth and drink out of it. I have known my father pick up pounds—pounds in this way, and get fuddled into the bargain. This must have been back in the old hunting days when the Honourable Newton Fellowes, Sir Arthur Chichester, and Squire Worth were the leaders. My father, of course, did not keep the head, which was taken after this performance to the place where the carcase had been left.

As regards schooling, I fear I cannot give much of an account of myself, being fond of "mitching" or playing truant, as the phrase is nowadays. Our schoolmaster was Old Keen ; and, no mistake, he *was* keen. Many in Dulverton can remember, or have heard of him as a big smart man, who shot, fished, and played the fiddle. For our feelings he cared nothing. On winter mornings, when the thermometer was degrees below zero, there was no fire ; and if we wished to warm ourselves, we had to bring a stick with us. Old Keen, too, kept a stick and used to warm us with it. Talk about warming, I've felt my hands tingle for hours ; and I don't

5

wonder that Mr William Fisher, who is eighty
years old, keeps his grandfather's clock set to
nine o'clock, just to remind himself that he has
no longer to toddle off to Fore Street, and risk
a flogging from that terrible schoolmaster.

After I left school, I started broom-making
with a companion, Tom Berry. We used to
make birchen brooms in Burridge Wood, on the
yonder side of the Barle, not every day, but
in and out, as it were. At that time almost
everybody made brooms, no ingenuity being
required ; and it was the regular trade of a blind
man at Bury. We lopped the big limb of a
birch tree, and cut off the sprouts. Then we
made binds of brambles, or, sometimes, red
withies. Setting up a knife on our knee, and
holding it fast, we drew the bramble across
so as to scrape out the pith and leave the skin.
The skin is tough, and strong, and therefore
well suited for a bind. In fact, hardly anything
will break it. Placing the sprouts in the binds,
we drew the binds tight, and then the stick
straight, not over big, and sharpened at the
point, was forced in. We were compelled to
sell to the shops, and, as the market price of
a broom was twopence, we had to content ourselves with three-halfpence, so as to enable the

6

shopkeepers to make a profit. Our principal customer was old Betty Reed, who kept a little huckster's shop, and sold, amongst other goods, red herring and "poor Jan,"—our Dulverton name for salt Newfoundland fish.

As broom-making did not pay, we drew lots which should be hanged. Two grass-mots of different lengths were used ; I drew the shorter. Thereupon Tom Berry put the rope round my neck, threw the end of it over the first limb of a birch tree, and pulled me off my legs. I turned black in the face, and Tom, getting nervous, let me down. I was then about fourteen.

Some time elapsed, and then I heard of the railway construction that was going on below Exeter. I resolved to try my luck, and, reaching Starcross, succeeded in obtaining employment. My job consisted in carrying mortar and tending masons on the sea-wall. The navvies were a rough lot, and amused themselves by egging me and another boy on to fight. Our encounters took place in the dinner hour, and while they laughed, we covered each other with blood. In more peaceable times, we made our way into Powderham Park, and took young cranes out of their nests. This was dangerous

7

sport. Anybody who knows about cranes is aware that they build their nests high, on the topmost boughs of trees ; and if either of us had slipped, it is pretty certain there would have been no more dinner fights. But, danger or no danger, up we went, seized the nestlings, carried them home, and ate them. They were not very good eating. To be palatable, cranes should be salted for two or three days so as to get the fishy taste out of them ; and this we neglected to do.

As a boy I was not partial to work, and it happened that a man employed on the works was of the same kidney. He belonged to Dulverton ; and, between us, we bought a dog. He was a noble-looking animal—a lurcher. Thinking that the dog was going to maintain us, we decided to shut up work and return home. Accordingly, we did so, walking from Exeter to avoid expense. The dog accompanied us. On nearing Dulverton we observed quite a dozen hares on Helverton Knap. My companion marked a particular hare, and held up the dog, which marked her too. Away flew the hare towards the wood, but the dog was too fast for her, caught her, and was bringing her back, when Graves, afraid of being detected, ran to

meet him.   After that I flattered myself I was
in for a fortune, as indeed I was—a small one.
From time to time we tried the dog, and were
successful in catching several hares.   The lurcher
had one peculiarity for which I never could
account.   It was this, that, though there might
be plenty of hares about, he would not enter the
same field twice.   At last we sold him to some
gipsies for a sovereign.

Before going further, I ask any sensible
person reading this book, what chance had I,
surrounded by such influences in my childhood
and 'teens, of not being a poacher?   I state this
question, not as one ashamed of his calling, but
only for argument sake.   It must be remembered
that fifty or sixty years ago, hard work did not
pay.   Farmers were bent on making money, and
if the labourer received seven shillings a week,
it was considered as much as he was worth.
The villages were bursting with folks.   Nearly
every cottage was clogged with boys and girls
growing up.   And they all had to live somehow.
The price of bread was high.   I have known
it up to thirteenpence a loaf.   As for butcher's
meat, it was an unheard-of luxury.   What was
more natural, then, than that puzzled chaps, with
no brains for making their way in the world,

should help themselves now and again to wild creatures, both birds and beasts? Things are different now, but if you had lived fifty or sixty years ago, and seen with my eyes, you might not be so hard on the poor poacher.

I say this in excuse for my friends, many of whom would have preferred to be honest. For myself, I admit candidly that I did not take to poaching as a means of livelihood, or, at least, as a means of livelihood solely. I liked poaching; I loved poaching; I was never so happy as when I was poaching. You see it was in my blood. I was a born poacher and a born rogue.

If it were not for this consideration, I should be tempted to hand myself down to fame as a public benefactor. Picture me in my prime going up through the streets, with my gun on my shoulder, and followed by a crowd of men out of work—married men with families—begging to be allowed to accompany me. Mind, these were not lazy fellows, but good workmen, who hated to stand about on the bridge with their hands in their pockets, and who knew nothing of poaching. With bread at a shilling a loaf, their case was pitiable, so sometimes I took one, sometimes another, and altogether I have been the means of feeding scores of them. Although they were not skilled in poaching, I have enabled them to earn no less than four shillings as their share, and that I call good pay for such services as they could render. So, you perceive, a poacher is not of necessity a hard-hearted bad man; he may have more of the milk of humankindness than many a "toff" piquing himself on his superior virtue.

Besides being a shoemaker and a poacher, my father was a bumbailiff. Once he had a distress at Exebridge, and he and I went down to take an inventory of all the goods in the house. That done, he, having other business at Dulverton, left me to watch the premises. This was generally my work, or, at least, it was supposed to be. As soon as I thought he was clear of the place, I stepped over to the Anchor, and, finding several people there, got drinking with them. And then we went out to play skittles. I stayed at the public till I was so-and-so. When night came, I returned to the cottage with the intention of going to bed, but lo and behold! the house was empty. The things were all gone, and the old man (he was a labourer) with them. I was dumfounded, and at first did not know what to do. "I'm bound to go home and tell father of it," I said to myself, but for a long time I could not make up my mind. I was afraid.

However, I had a drop of liquor in my head, and that, I suppose, helped me along a bit, putting more spirit, more devil into me than I should otherwise have had. When I told father, he said,

"You've done a pretty thing, to let the man take away all the things."

I could not deny it; I had.

He put on his hat, and set off for Exebridge, but I was too frightened to accompany him. Some time in the night he came back, and I heard him say to mother,

"Everything is gone."

I cannot tell how ashamed I felt. I was seventeen or eighteen at the time—almost as good a man as I am now, and certainly old enough to know better.

"Don't say too much to the boy," answered mother, "or perhaps he'll enlist as a soldier." (I was a sort of dollymop, or favourite.)

"Well, there," he said, "I don't know what I shall do about it."

He considered for some time, and then added,

"I suppose I must send word to the landlord,

and tell him that there were not things enough to pay my expenses, and those of the auctioneer."

And that was how I got out of the scrape.

The old man must have been pretty dapper, as he succeeded in removing, amongst other property, bags of potatoes. But he had several neighbours, and all hung together like an ounce of rag-'baccy. Not one of them would give information, and there is little doubt that he got help from them. Be that as it may, the lesson was not lost on me, as my next incident will show.

It happened that we had three distresses at Withypool—all in one day. I may observe in passing that distresses were frequent in those days ; they were always happening. Well, my father, and brother, and I set off for Withypool, which, as you may know, is a village some eight miles from Dulverton. First we repaired to a little dairy place kept by one "Tisser" Wilson. Father took down the names of all the things to serve as a list for the auctioneer, and, as before, left me to mount guard. It was our practice to remain for five days, and at the end of the five days came the sale. No sooner was father gone than the old woman, who had received us, asked me to have some cream and jam.

"Thank you, ma'am," I answered.

So she kept stuffing me with it; in fact, I could not have enough. After a while I missed the old woman, and she did not return for quite half-an-hour. A few minutes later another old woman entered.

"Oh, excuse me, Mrs Wilson," she said, "I wants that washing-tub I lent 'ee t'other day."

"You can't have it," I said, "the washing-tub's marked." I had seen enough washing-tubs at Exebridge to answer my purpose.

"Well, but," she protested, "it's very hard for me to lose my washing-tub."

"Can't help it," I replied. "I'm not going to spare it, and you had no business to lend it."

Not many minutes elapsed before another old woman appeared.

"Mrs Wilson!" she cried, "I wants that butter-tub I lent 'ee."

"No use," I said, thinking once more of Exebridge, "the butter-tub's marked."

She muttered something about its being very bad.

"Never mind, missus!" I answered, cheerfully.

Will it be believed? in a very little while another old woman popped in.

14

HOW I WENT ON WHEN A BOY

"Mrs Wilson!"

"Yes."

"I want that boiler I lent 'ee t'other day."

"The boiler's marked," I said.

"What, be going to sell it?"

"Yes," was my reply, "if the rent isn't paid by such and such a time." Legally, I was supposed to have my warrant and produce it, if called on. However, nothing was said about that.

"Well, this is a fine thing," she continued. "To think that after I have been so kind as to lend the boiler, I can't have it again!"

"Can't help it," I said.

To cut my story short, the rent was paid in a day or two, but, as punishment for refusing to oblige, I was not offered any more bread and cream.

On another occasion we went to a little farm called Pinkery in Oakford parish to take a distress for rent. Father made a tour of the premises, marking the things—drags, harrows, a plough, an old horse, etc.—and, in doing so, observed a beautiful fat pig in the "loose." The farmer said he hadn't any meat in the house, and begged me to ask father to have the pig killed and put in the salter. Of course

you know that, while the animal might have
been sold alive, bailiffs are not allowed to take
eatables or clothing. Well, I kept bumming
father, and at last he said,

"Poor fellow, I suppose we must."

We heated the water to scald the pig and get
the hair off, and the old man killed it. Next
morning it was cut up, and salted in. I ought
to add that father knew there was sufficient to
pay the rent, without the pig, so that nobody
was the worse for our indulgence.

When I worked with my father shoemaking,
he could not get me to do anything to the
bottoms of them. I wanted to be the master-
stitcher; it was hard work to sew bottoms.
However, he never ceased to pester me on the
subject, while I remained obstinate and refused
to obey his wishes. At last he persuaded me
that the best plan would be for me to leave
and "learn out" the trade with somebody else.
About this time the annual revel was held at
Anstey or Old Way's End, and, of course, I
must attend. No revel would have been complete if I were not present. Whilst there I
met with a shoemaker of Withypool, called
Crudge, and we got into conversation. I may
say in passing that there were any number of

shoemakers in the villages then ; in these days
of ready-made boots, that is no longer the case.
Well, this man asked me what I could do
towards shoemaking, as he wanted help. I told
him that I could stitch the uppers, whereupon
he said,

"You come with me for twelve months at
three shillings a week and your meat, and I'll
learn you out the trade."

I agreed, the understanding being that I was
to present myself on the Monday morning
following. It happened that on that day a
shoemaker of Dulverton was going to Winsford
very early, and we set off together. My companion's name was Thorn, and, as he is still
living, he can confirm my story. When we
reached the spot—Spire Cross—where our ways
parted, I said to him,

"You may as well go on to Withypool along
with me. I'll give you something to drink
when we get there."

I could afford to promise that, as I had been
a teetotaller for several months, and had three
pounds in my pocket. Thorn consented to
accompany me, and I arrived at Mr Crudge's
before they had had breakfast. Entering the
house, I spoke to the master and the missus and

the men, for he had two or three hands working for him.

"Suppose you want breakfast, coming so far," said Mr Crudge. "We haven't been to breakfast our own selves yet."

I offered no objection, and sat down. Presently the men left the room for the kitchen, where I observed a lot of basins on the table, and a great crock suspended over the fire. In a minute or two they began to dip broth out of the crock with a ladle, at the same time calling to me,

"Come in and sit down to breakfast along with the rest."

I got over to my broth, tasted a spoonful or two, and then paused to reflect. Thought I to myself, "I can't eat it."

"Do you get this every morning?" I whispered to one of the fellows.

"Yes," he answered.

"I can never get through all these broths," I thought. "To do so would take at least a month out of the year. If there's to be broth every morning, I ain't going to have it." Nor would you. Mind it was not chicken broth, nor mutton broth, but always salt-pork broth with leeks and bread. For a long time I didn't say

anything, but kept "studying," and the general
tenor of my thoughts was this—that it wasn't a
bit like the living that I'd been accustomed to—
roast pheasant, jugged hare, and venison fresh
or salt. After a while I left my broth, informing
the master that I wished to go down to the
public-house to see my friend. This in effect I
did. Having related my experiences, I told him
that I had fully considered the matter and did
not believe in learning to work hard.

"Please yourself," was his reply.

I followed this advice and did not return to
the shoemaker's, but stayed about almost all the
day at the public-house. One of the things I
disliked at Mr Crudge's was that there was only
a turf-fire. In fact, I felt miserable the moment
I entered the house.

In the evening Thorn was obliged to set out
for Winsford, and I accompanied him. On
arriving, the man he worked for asked me to
stay and help fit some boots that week, and I
agreed. But bless me! if I did not exactly
jump from the frying-pan into the fire, at any
rate I did not better myself. Broth again!
However, I thought I would put up with it till
the Saturday, when I should be able to go
home with my mate. At the end of the week I

trudged back to Dulverton with the firm resolve
to throw up the whole concern. Where was the
sense, I argued, of sitting with nose and knees
together shoemaking, whilst there was plenty
of stuff flying and running about the country?
So I went back to my old ways.

CHAPTER II

I BEGIN TO POACH IN EARNEST

THE next step in my career as a poacher was the purchase of a gun. I recollect all about it. I bought a barrel for eighteen-pence—the same price as the fellow in the rhyme paid for a fiddle—and took it to Bishop's Nympton to have a stock fitted to it. There was living in the village a wheelwright sort of chap, to whom I explained my errand, and he told me to call again in a fortnight. At the fortnight's end, with an ounce of powder, a pound of shot, and a hap'orth of caps, I set off to fetch my gun. I found all in readiness, and having paid my money, felt, you may believe, proud enough. On the way back a curlew passed; I shot, and killed it. Carrying it home, I showed it to a number of people, after which I took it to a tradesman of the town who was nearly blind. I suppose he could not distinguish properly; anyhow, I sold the bird for a woodcock, and received half-a-crown for it. This seemed to me an excellent beginning, and I was highly delighted in consequence.

Time went on ; the passion—poaching is like gambling—grew stronger and stronger. I killed a hare in Execleave, and then pheasants, rabbits, hares, anything. Poaching was more profitable than work at the low wages then offered ; and the pleasure and excitement of the thing suited my constitution. At last, I began to consider that I was old enough to go out with father night-hunting. I acquainted him with my wish, and, as he was agreeable, often accompanied him in his expeditions. For a time all went well, but it was not long before we got snapped.

We had been over Lord Carnarvon's grounds on Bury Hill, and, after being out all night, were on our way home. We had gone as far as Hele Bridge when all at once I found I was a net short. It was clear that, by some accident, one had been left behind. Father sent my brother and me back for it, while he himself took the load of nine hares, and, followed by the dog, went on again towards Dulverton. The notion was that, by separating, we should avoid all risk in the event of capture. However, Bill and I went back, and were half-way up the field in which, it was supposed, the net had been left, when, in a low tone, my brother remarked:

"There's someone up there, smoking."

I could not believe it, and tried to encourage him. It was no use. His confidence had been shaken, and he would go no further. I went up to the gateway alone. No sooner had I picked up the net than out jumped sixteen of 'em on me, crying,

"We've got the beggars."

Taken utterly by surprise, and almost frightened to death, I yelled ten thousand murders, but the next moment recollected myself and halloa'd a warning to my brother. Poor old father, of course, the staff of the house, had gone home.

"Look sharp there!" rang a voice. "There's more about."

Down some of them ran, and discovered my brother sitting inside a gate. As the field was crossed by a public path, he deemed himself, quite wrongly, secure. The keepers took us to the house of a man called Westacott, at Hele Bridge, and regaled us with a breakfast of eggs, bacon, and fried potatoes.

In the meantime they sent to Dulverton for the constables. Whilst we waited, the keepers began to chaff brother Bill, because he had fallen into their hands. Under the circumstances, this was more than he could stand; and, being a pretty smart fellow, he knocked three or four of 'em down. In due course, the constables arrived and escorted us into Dulverton to be tried. As we were going down through the town, we met a party of stag-hunters, several of whom were justices. In one way they were perhaps almost as reluctant as we were, but they had to stop and hear the case. Mr Gough, Lord Carnarvon's head-steward, appeared to prosecute, and the magistrates' decision was three months' imprisonment apiece. In addition, we had to find bail for twelve months' good behaviour.

As I wish always to remember acts of kindness, and have never borne malice against stewards, keepers, constables, or justices for anything they may have done in the discharge of their duty, it is with pleasure that I record Mr Gough's good-natured intercession on behalf of us poor boys. As far as he knew, it was our first offence, and he begged off a month for us.

It was the custom sometimes to march prisoners to the county jail, a distance of twenty miles. We rode to Taunton in a cart,

I BEGIN TO POACH IN EARNEST

but felt very dismal. People in those days wore their hair long. We brothers had beautiful hair—Bill, particularly—and one of our chief regrets in going to prison was the necessity of being shorn. Apart from that, my brother was more fortunate than I. He was a tailor, and got into the tailors' shop. I, on the other hand —poor devil!—had to tread the wheel, with the exception of Sundays, seven hours a day. This I felt rather sharp. With regard to diet, we had a pint of skilly, and half-a-pound of bread for breakfast. Dinner consisted of a pint of soup, a pound of potatoes, three ounces of beef and half-a-pound of bread. Supper was a repetition of breakfast. We rose at six and went to bed at six. On the expiration of our sentence, home, and at the poaching again!

This was all I intended to say about prison-life on this occasion, but one or two particulars have occurred to me, which, I think, may interest people who have no knowledge or experience of such matters. First, I may mention that, when prisoners walked to prison, they were allowed seven shillings—the equivalent of trap-hire. Generally they did the whole distance, over twenty miles, in one day, but I remember that for some reason—owing probably to our

starting late—I once got no further than
Wiveliscombe, where I was handed over by
the Dulverton policeman to his Wiveliscombe
brother, Lacy Collard.

Those were the early days of the county
constabulary, and the members of the force
certainly did not err on the side of leniency.
Lacy Collard, in particular, was absurdly severe.
When bedtime came, the old man took me up
to his room, and made me lie on the floor, on the
bare planks, with my hand-bolts on. He, for
his part, retired into the seclusion of a comfortable old-fashioned four-poster, where there was
lots of room for me, if Collard had only had the
good grace to invite me to share it with him.
Instead of doing so, he took in his staff—a
clear proof that he was afraid of me. Now,
if one thing is more certain than another, it is
that I ought to have teased that old fellow all
night, but I thought I might as well go along
quietly, and get back to the prison—the old
shop—as quickly as possible.

Before going to the treadmill you were ex-
amined, stripped like a recruit, and if you
were a healthy subject, the doctor would report
of you, "This man's sound; he's fit for the
wheel."

26

I BEGIN TO POACH IN EARNEST

You qualified for this examination by washing, having your hair cut, and donning a prison-suit—a short round jacket with no pockets, coarse dark breeches, and shoes. As I had a pretty good leg, the breeches fastened tight and served as a pocket for 'baccy. The cap was in shape not unlike an old nightcap, but it was knitted. We wore also an odd little necktie with two strings.

Billy Dinner, the chief warder, was a hard-hearted, sarcastic old fellow. When the time came for us to go on the treadmill, he would enter and say, " Come, my little lads, be ready. There's a beautiful instrument—a pianner—out here for you to play with." But when we came to it, we found that it was not a fingering, but a treading, instrument. Then Old Billy's tone would change, and he would say sternly,

" Go and tread that for seven hours."

And tread it we did, with the exception of two and a half minutes' rest every twenty minutes. On the first day, however, about eleven o'clock you might be called off the wheel to see the parson, and he would have a dialogue with you for your good.

" What are you here for ? " he would ask.

AUTOBIOGRAPHY OF A POACHER

"Only a bit of poaching."

"Ah, but," he would say, "poaching leads to other things. First a hare, next a fowl, next sheep-stealing, next highway robbery, next murder!"

His words, I confess, made a considerable impression on me, though I felt that I had to go through a good many rubs before I came to murder. However, I know that there was much sense in his remarks, and it is quite possible that they checked me in my downward course—except as regards poaching. No prison-chaplain on earth could have cured me of that.

The wheel of the treadmill was of wood, and farmers, labourers, and people of the town brought grists to be ground. If there was no corn, we called the process grinding wind, but we much preferred to grind corn, as then the wheel went slower.

The night after I came back from prison an incident occurred which, though trivial, may still be recorded as showing the alarms to which poachers are subject. I was in want of money, and my father and I decided to go out night-hunting. Bill was not at home; he was up at King's Brompton, tailoring. Hares were anywhere in those days, so we made for a field just outside Battleton Wood. When we got to Beesley ground, we tried the field. Father went round to till the nets to the gates, while I stood at the lower gate prepared to let go the dog. We could depend on that dog, he was a proper night-hunting dog, so when he came back, after I had let him go, and told me there was nothing there, I believed him. Taking up my net, I went round to the gates, expecting to meet with father, but could not find him. Again I went round, and again could not find him. At last, I went home.

Although Bill was away, several sisters were living in the house, as, of course, was my mother. I could not hide from them my concern. Except on one supposition I could make neither head nor tail of it. If he had been caught, most probably I should have been caught too. The explanation did not lie, it would seem, in *that* direction. What, then? It was a dreadful mode of accounting for his absence, but it appeared to me most likely that he was dead. He suffered from palpitations.

There was pretty consternation at Duck Paddle. The old woman, when I told her, rose and laid in the fire, and we all sat up till daylight, scarcely saying a word, and shivering with fear and anxiety. Just as it began to dawn, he walked in, and glad enough we were to see him. He informed us that he had fallen asleep, which was no wonder, considering that he had been out two or three nights following, besides cobbling by day. If I had been a little more experienced, this solution would probably have occurred to me. Often since then I have slept walking on the road from King's Brompton, and fancied I heard something. This was my brother, also asleep, while poor old father, himself barely awake, trudged along after. You would think it hardly possible for people to be so done up, but it is, and I have proved it.

Before I proceed to my next story, I think it proper to relate how I came by my title. If you walked with me through the streets of Dulverton, you would notice that very few, and those comparative strangers, address me by my surname. Instead of "Good morning, Mr Holcombe," it is "Well, John," or still oftener, "Well, Lordy." If I am spoken of behind my back, it is as "his Lordship," or "Lord Mansfield." Perhaps you will like me to explain. It was all along, as we say, of an old song. Several of us drunkards were at the New

I BEGIN TO POACH IN EARNEST

Inn, when somebody proposed that I should sing. I knew one ditty that I had learnt of some old fellow—I cannot remember whom—and gave it. It was a highwayman's song; and, although I have forgotten one or two of the verses, was roughly as follows :—

In Scotland I was bred and born,
And Saffern (or Stafford) Green brought me to scorn.
'Twas there I learnt a baking trade ;
They called me a wild and a roving blade.

Then for London I bore away,
Spending my time in ball and play,
Until my cash it did run low,
On the highways I was forced to go.

I took a kind and a loving wife,
I loved her as dear as I love my life ;
And to maintain her both fine and gay,
To all the world my life I'll pay.

I robb'd Lord Mansfield, I do declare,
And left him on St James's Square ;
I bade him good-night and the best of cheer,
While I ran to spoil with my comrades dear.

I oftentimes used to resort
To Hounslow Heath and St James's Park,
Where I robb'd both lords and ladies bright.
Five hundred pounds I won that night.

Then for Scotland I bore away,
To see my dear wife so fine and gay,
Until Blind Fielding did me pursue,
And taken I was by that bloody crew.

31

AUTOBIOGRAPHY OF A POACHER

I wish I'd hearken'd to my friends' advice,
And left off drinking, gaming, cards, and dice.
But I robbed the rich, and I did bestow
What I stole from them on the poor and low.

Then I was taken to the justice hall,
Where I was forced to stand before great and small.
Sergeant John Bagwell did me commit,
And straight to Newgate I was sent.

When I came to the fatal tree,
Many a fair one did mourn for me.
No sighs nor tears they won't save me,
Nor keep me from that fatal tree.

Now I am dead, pray let me have
Six brisk young women to carry me to my grave,
Six brisk young women to bear up my pall ;
Give them white gowns and pink ribbons all,
That they may say when I'm in my grave,
" There goes a wild and ɔ roving blade."

Well, as I said, I first sang this song at the
New Inn, Dulverton. There happened to be
sitting by me one Bryant, a tailor and a bugler
in the cavalry, who named me, after one of
the verses, " Lord Mansfield " ; and, whether
well or ill bestowed, the title has stuck to me
ever since. Of one thing I am certain, and
I doubt not most of my readers will agree, I
have "*apropos'd*" my song, even to the hanging.
Singularly enough, I am not the first of my
family to be ennobled. My father's mother's

brother was old King Holcombe.[1] I suppose
he went by the name of King Holcombe because he was the biggest farmer at Hawkridge,
where he lived at Zeal Farm, under Lord
Carnarvon, and kept a lot of sheep. He being
a king, and I being a lord, I hold that I've
a vein or two of royal blood ; in fact, I always
consider my blood to be of two different
colours. That's what made me so fond of the
royal game, the royal venison.

For all that he was a king, Holcombe, like
many other farmers, dressed roughly. He
wore breeches and stockings, no gaiters. I
have known a farmer wear kerseymeres to
church. Very little cloth was to be seen, but
there were plenty of velvets, all down through.
Although there was no high living in those
days, I was fond of going up to Hawkridge.
When I got there the old woman would make
me a basin of whit-pot, very acceptable after
my long walk. Whit-pot was a substitute for
bread, of which there was not much going.
You put water in a pot and made it boil.

---

[1] I can confirm this statement from Mr Boyse's memoranda
(see Collyns, *Chase of the Wild Red Deer*, p. 219).

   "August 26th, 1813.—The hounds met at Hawkridge, where
old farmer Holcombe, better known as the King of Hawkridge,
reported a good stag to be in Ashway Hat."—CARACTACUS.

Then you took flour, salt, and milk, and stirred
them up in a dish or great basin with cold
water. Cold, not hot, otherwise the ingredients
would clog. You kept stirring, and, as you
did so, threw the mixture little by little into
the hot water until the dish was empty. Then
it would be served up. On coming away my
great-aunt would give me a pudding or chunk
of cheese to carry home to my father. Cheese
in our neighbourhood was very hard, and you
almost required a wedge and mallet to cleave
it abroad.

King Holcombe was unmarried, and the old
woman I spoke of was his sister, who kept
house for him. The story I am about to
relate has mainly to do with her. The Lord
Carnarvon of the day used sometimes to go
up Hawkridge way—I say "up," since it is
one of the highest and coldest spots round
Dulverton—poult-shooting, and one day he
arranged to call at Zeal for lunch. Just before
lunch time—this is what my father told me—
my great-aunt remembered something.

"Drat the maid!" she cried, meaning the
parish apprentice, "we must make haste. But
we haven't got a table-cloth. Never mind,
go and take out a clean bed-sheet. Do very

34

well. His Lordship will make no difference
of it."

It was a funny sort of table-cloth for Lord
Carnarvon, but I never heard that any remarks
were passed. In those days table-cloths were
very rare in farmhouses. People were more
homely, and farmers did not keep hunters as
they do now.

I must now go back to the New Inn. This
public was a favourite resort of mine, and I
cannot accurately recollect whether the ensuing
adventure took place on the same or a different
occasion from the evening above referred to.
Be that as it may, there was a good muster
present, and they and I had been drinking.
No doubt I was a bit elevated, and, being in
that state, offered to bet that I would go and
kill a hare and return within an hour. No
sooner offered than taken. I left the house,
forged my way up High Street, past the Rock,
and on to the Jewry plantation. I failed to
find my hare, and, rather crestfallen, turned
towards home, when—presto !—something happened.

It appeared that, unknown to myself, two
keepers were waiting for me. The instant I
jumped over the gate into the road they

collared me, and I was told that I should have to go with them to Pixton, and give a report of myself to Squire Bisset.

This gentleman was a great man in our corner of the world, being Master of the Devon and Somerset Staghounds, and a sworn enemy of poachers, especially deer-poachers. He certainly, neither then nor at any time, showed me the slightest favour, and I had every reason to look upon him as a personal foe. As, however, all this happened so long ago, and he is dead and gone, I have no objection to say that he was as fine a man as has been seen in our country. Tremendously heavy—one of the heaviest men that ever rode hunting—but active and good all through; I confess, if he had laid his grip on me I should have found it impossible to get away. But he left this sort of work to police and keepers, and always demeaned himself as a gentleman.

I walked along the high road a prisoner. The keepers, one on each side, held me by the collar, and the more I reflected on the situation the less I liked it. Suddenly I gave a spring, broke free, and ran off towards Dulverton. As fortune would have it, they had with them a big mastiff, and him they let slip.

I BEGIN TO POACH IN EARNEST

The dog was muzzled, but it was in vain for me to try to make headway, as he kept beating me down with his paws.

"Well, John, he's stopped you," said the keepers, laughing. "You'll have to go to Pixton after all."

And so I had. I have thought since that, as they were men six foot high, and strong in proportion, they could have held me all right, but they wanted to see some sport with the dog. By-and-by we arrived at Pixton House, and they invited me in to see Mr Bisset. I was forced to comply. After a few moments the keepers retired to speak to their master, turned the key on me, and left me alone in the kitchen. It happened that in the cupboard was some beer. To this I helped myself, and whilst I was so engaged all three entered and caught me. However, little notice was taken of that. Mr Bisset was in evening dress. I think I see him now, with his great frame, light hair, and fair complexion. But to me he was anything but gracious. His tone was stern and his manner contemptuous.

"Ah!" said he to the keepers, "so you've got him, and a good job, too!"

By this time I was half-drunk, and, as I did

37

not relish being spoken of in that way, lost control of myself and called him all kinds of names. The politest thing I said to him was that he ought to have been a "navigator." This was not intended as a compliment, though, had he been less angry, he might, perhaps, have taken it as such. The squire, however, was in no humour for jesting.

"Let him go," he said, again addressing the keepers, "but watch him out of the park. He'll hear more of it."

So it proved. I was summoned for trespassing in pursuit, and rewarded with a month's imprisonment. The sentence was undeniably light, but would no doubt have been heavier, had it not been for the fact that the offence occurred on the edge of the evening. Trespass of that sort was not like night-hunting.

In my next exploit three of us were implicated. Marley was a little splinter-shinned chap, a tailor, who used to wear a box-hat and a swallow-tail coat. To see him, you would never have believed he was a poacher, but he was, and, what is more, the clothes were not more innocent than the man. For instance, his box-hat—when he was out poaching, he would bestow a pheasant or two in it. So if you

I BEGIN TO POACH IN EARNEST

knocked off his hat, you knocked off a brace
of pheasants. As for Harry Liscombe, he was
a sawyer, and a fine fellow, but I could never
persuade myself that he had much heart.
Well, one afternoon, Marley, Liscombe, and
myself, set off from Dulverton and went out
wiring on Sir Thomas Acland's allotment,
close by the keeper's lodge on Winsford Hill.
I suppose there is no need to explain what
wiring is. A wire is formed into a noose, or
running knot, which binds the closer the more
it is drawn. These snares are placed in the
creeps; pheasants walk into them, and get
hanged.

We had tilled up our wires round the fences
when the suspicion seized us that there was
a man creeping about, and that he had seen
our activity. However, our suspicion was not
confirmed, and, as it was now evening, we
went home. The next morning we were out
on the hill before it was light, and looking
across the field in which our wires had been
left. Again it seemed to us as if there were
a man creeping about in the furze. This time
all doubt on the subject was removed. After
a while the fellow got numb, and so was forced
to rise and show himself.

AUTOBIOGRAPHY OF A POACHER

"There!" said Marley, "I told you they were watching us."

"Let's move on, and get out of this," I said.

We walked off up the hill.

We had not gone far when, on looking back, we saw we were being pursued. The enemy, seven or eight in number, were nimble chaps, and soon overtook us. I was the first to be pounced on, being seized by two men who told me that breakfast was waiting for me down at Winsford. The same intimation was conveyed to my companions. When we reached the village, we found, sure enough, a good breakfast provided for us by Mr Paul of the Royal Oak. It was their intention, as soon as breakfast was over, to bring us before a gentleman who was at once parson and magistrate.

On inquiry, it turned out that Mr Mitchell was not at home. So we stayed on drinking at the Royal Oak till two o'clock, when we were treated to an excellent dinner of fried meat and beer, as much as we cared to have. No doubt, this was a precaution, to keep us quiet. Soon after the announcement was made that Mr Mitchell had returned, whereupon we all adjourned to the vicarage. The

magistrate began by examining the keepers.
He asked them what they had seen. This
was a poser. Not one of them had seen us
touch any wire; and, to cut matters short,
they could not give satisfactory answers.
However, we were told we were suspicious
characters, and ought to be had up as rogues
and vagabonds for wandering about the
country. Mr Mitchell then turned to Tailor
Marley.

"What were you doing there?" he demanded.

"Please, sir, I'm asthmatical," was the reply,
"and I was gathering a little agrimony and
wood-betony for my complaint."

"Humbug!" said the magistrate.

One was enough for that job, not three,
and that Mr Mitchell knew. Still, there was
no real evidence against us, and therefore
he had no choice but to dismiss the case and
allow us to return to the public. No victuals
or beer this time. It was "Go about your
business!" Finding that we could get no
drink, and having no money, we left. On the
whole, we had not done badly. We had consumed not less than forty quarts of beer,
besides breakfast and dinner; and for all this
Sir Thomas had the privilege of paying. To

complete our success, a few wires had been tilled at Leigh, and on our way back we found two pheasants hitched up to them. These we appropriated, made a good price of them, and spent the money in carousing at the Nightingale in Lady Street, of which Bryant was the landlord—the man who named me Lord Mansfield. So ended that exploit.

Although I shall be going out of my way chronologically—I think it is called — I am tempted to relate another incident that occurred on the same spot. Another man and myself had been up wiring on Sir Thomas's property. We had laid down the wires in the afternoon, and early on the following morning repaired to the spot—it was at Leigh—to ascertain the result. In the first wire we found a dead cat. I was stooping down to extricate her when I heard a sudden noise, and, bustling through the hedge, appeared three or four farmers. They were great fellows, six foot high, called Norman, and, like other farmers on the estates, were bound to assist in looking after their landlord's interests. Well, there it was—only a cat, but our intention was plain. We were summoned, convicted, and sentenced to a fine of three pounds nine shillings apiece, or, as an alternative, two months' imprisonment. This seemed to me pretty sharp doctrine, and I was in favour of going to prison. My mate, however, objected. He had been in jail before, and had not enjoyed the experience.

"But how are you going to find the money?" I asked.

"I will pawn my bed towards some of it," he replied.

And so he did. I, on my part, pawned as many things as I could get hold of; and, between us, we scraped together enough to pay the fine. But it was a terrible expense, and all, you might say, for the sake of a cat!

CHAPTER III

I EXPERIENCE BAD LUCK, AND UNKNOWINGLY ENLIST (?)

MY next adventure took place on the eve of Dulverton Fair. Two fairs were held at Dulverton—the summer and the winter. This was the winter fair. Now I and one of my mates, talking together, considered that we had not enough money for the occasion, and resolved to get more. As it turned out, instead of going to the fair, we went to prison, but more of that presently. Off we started for Withiel Florey, a distance of six miles, on a visit to Squire Lethbridge's property. It was about "dimpse" when we arrived, and we entered a plantation just as the birds were going up to roost. I noticed three which were, I believe, hen-pheasants.

"It is time we began to shoot," said my comrade.

"No!" I answered, "the men on the estate are only just leaving work."

However, he was persistent, and at last I

44

I EXPERIENCE BAD LUCK

shot one and picked it up. A moment later
I heard a lot of fellows coming. It was clear
they had been watching us. There was only
one thing to do—we began to run. On we
went to the wood-hedge, and climbed over into
a field.

"Let's get in here," said my comrade, "and
hide away in the ditch-trough."

"No!" I answered, again showing my wisdom.
"Better to keep running."

"If we do, we shall be sure to be caught," he
protested.

It was rather whispering than talking, but
I could see that he was in earnest, and for the
second time I allowed myself to be overruled.
We lay down in the ditch-trough, he under,
I on top. By-and-by they came into the field,
and missed us. Surprised and disappointed,
they cursed and swore, but in a moment or
two somebody suggested,

"Tread back that ditch-trough."

This they accordingly did, and a great
hulking chap trod on my back. "Glorious
sound! Here the beggars are!" And the
whole crew were wild with joy. They were
nothing but a rough dunghill set of fellows,
and appeared to have mistaken me for a cer-

tain Jack Takle. They forced us to go with them across the bottom to the keeper's cottage, where we were detained. Meanwhile some of the party proceeded to Luxborough. After a time two constables arrived. They were in their own clothes, and had been chosen, as was the custom in those days and in those parts, by the farmers. Nevertheless, they were Queen's men, and we were bound to respect their authority. They and the keepering chaps escorted us to Chargot Lodge and arraigned us before the gentleman. They told him what we had done, after which they marched us to a public-house at Luxborough, supplied us with supper, and put us to bed. Next morning, a jolly good ten miles' ride to Wiveliscombe, in a horse and trap, to be tried!

On being placed in the dock, we pleaded not guilty, and put in a claim for legal advice. This was granted, and, to pay 'Torney Waldron his guinea, my mate pawned his watch. The main facts were beyond dispute, and neither of us hoped for an acquittal. Our object in employing a solicitor was to get the charge reduced, and to have it brought in as day instead of night work, as that would have meant a fine only. However, the keepers proved that the misbehaviour took place after sunset, and the magistrates imposed a sentence of three months' "choky" at Taunton. After that, good-bye to Dulverton Fair!

Luckily, when I was lodged in jail, I found I had fallen on good times. It happened that the premises were being enlarged, and I was sent out to help the masons. Making mortar and scraping bricks was better than my former experience—the treadmill; and, still more acceptable, I was allowed a pint of beer a day. When I entered the prison, I had a number of threepenny bits concealed in my mouth. With these I bought tobacco through the ordinary workmen, who were Taunton chaps. A score of us prisoners slept in one room, and we had jolly sprees, smoking by night what we had chewed by day. We used to wrestle, too, and beat each other with the pillows, to make them soft. Pleasant as this change was, we were really only making a rod for our own back. When I next made the acquaintance of Taunton Jail, I was put in a little hole, a separate cell, and, as a friend of mine expresses it, "sorrows began."

Let me see—when was it that I next entered the portals of the prison? Oh, I remember.

AUTOBIOGRAPHY OF A POACHER

I was up for a bit of night-hunting, so, accompanied by a friend, I started off for the hills. He was a young fellow, who had not done much poaching, and was, in fact, learning of me. We crossed Court Down, and reached a place called Bumper's Hill, about half-way between Dulverton and Winsford. There, in the first field tried, I tilled a net against the hedge. Hardly was this done when I heard footsteps approaching. I caught up the net, called in the dog, and walked along the road, where I deemed myself secure. As it happened, I ran right into the arms of a policeman called Edmonds.

"Holloa, John!" said he, "what are you doing here this time of night?"

"Oh, just having a bit of a stroll," I replied.

"Well," he observed, "I must search you."

"What right have you to search me?" I asked. "I've nothing but what belongs to me, and we're on the highway."

But search me he did, and took out two or three nets. During the conversation the other chap ran away, keeping the right side of the hedge.

"I'm sorry, John," said Edmonds, "but, of

course, you must expect to hear more about this."

"Oh, very well," I answered ; and, with that, we gave up for the night and returned home.

When morning came, I thought I would not trouble them to summon me, and made up my mind to go off. Just then Netley Hospital was in course of erection, and one of my brothers was employed at the works. Here then, it seemed, was my best chance of escape. I rode into Tiverton by post, and took ticket to Southampton. On reaching my destination, I walked out to Netley, saw my brother, and he got me work as a mason's slave. I forget what my wages were exactly—possibly fifteen shillings a week. I worked on steadily for a few days, and then the old fever came over me. I made inquiries whether there was any game about, and found that there was—any amount. So I bought an old carbine, with which I used to slip out night-times, and kill two or three pheasants. As, however, the carbine was made for balls, I was forced to go terribly close in order to kill them. So things went on until my brother, who shared my adventures, grew tired and afraid of being caught. He was a painter, earning something like thirty shillings a week, and the loss of such a job would have been a consideration. Then I picked up with another chap. He was a funny-looking fellow, an Irishman. There were plenty of his countrymen employed on the works, and some of them lodged in the same house as myself. This was a beer-shop, six or seven miles from Southampton, and close to the scene of our labours. Amongst other patrons of the establishment were several foremen, one of whom had a percussion gun that was fired with a cap.

"I'll lend it to you, if you like," he said.

"Thank you," I replied, only too pleased at the offer. But I was doomed to disappointment. On going out and trying it, I found it would not knock the birds dead, and was obliged to return to the old carbine. So things went on, without any particular incident, till one night I lost my mate. He had been caught in the act of stealing boards, and taken to Southampton. A few days afterwards the magistrates rewarded him for his dishonesty by a sentence of four months' imprisonment, and I began to think that it was about time I jacked up that kind of work. I did not like thievery, and would have nothing to do with stealing poultry, or stealing boards. As Paddy indulged in these evil practices, I came to the conclusion that he was too rough a character to take about with me.

There are those that say that, if a man poaches, he does not mind what he takes. Dr Collyns maintained this, and I have copied a passage out of his book, just to show you what was thought about poachers, and how little that kind-hearted gentleman was inclined to distinguish between good sort of men like me, and mere common thieves like that Paddy.

"A few years ago, when the deer inhabited the Brendon coverts in greater numbers than at present, many a good stag was destroyed by the poacher's hand. The heads were sold in Lynton and Lynmouth, and probably at this moment adorn the 'villas' of some respectable cheese-mongers or grocers, or other choice spirits of cockneydom. Pity it is that the proud owners of the coveted trophies should be ignorant of the fate of those labouring men who, by *their* instigation, and by the promise of *their* gold, were induced to become poachers. The offence when discovered (and it could not be kept secret) was not likely to be overlooked by a well-disposed farmer, who prided himself on being able to show the country a deer upon his land. The man

AUTOBIOGRAPHY OF A POACHER

who would kill a stag for gold, would, it was
argued, soon be brought to doubt the immorality of slaughtering a sheep, without any
strict regard to the difference between *meum*
and *tuum*, and the exodus of many a man who
might have lived and died in the parish in
which he was born and reared, was the consequence of the thoughtless and foolish selfish-
ness of those who, by the chink of a guinea,
lured to ruin and disgrace the rustic who was
all too poor and too weak to resist temptation.

"'Budaeus,' says Manwood, 'reporteth this
old verse of venison :

'Non est inquirendum unde venit venison,
Nam si forte furto sit, sola fides sufficit.'

"'If any one chance to be bid to his friend's
house to eat his part of fat venison, let him
remember this old verse, which in English is
this :

'It is not to be inquired from whence venison cometh,
For if by chance it stolen be
A good belief sufficeth thee.'

"Let me beg visitors to the West to avoid
following this advice."

Concerning Dr Collyns and stags I shall
have something to say presently. In the

I EXPERIENCE BAD LUCK

meantime I wish to express my dissent from the assertion that poaching leads to sheep-stealing, and mixing up what belongs to you with what doesn't. I am no great scholar, and a great deal of what the doctor wrote is Greek to me, but I can see clearly enough that that is the drift of the passage. " If you poach, most likely you steal, or soon will, and then you will perish and come to a fearful end." I grant this is an old saying, but it is not invariably correct. I have been out with that sort, but I have always steadily refused to be a party to their proceedings. Rabbits, for instance, were not worth the risk. A fine thing to shoot at a fourpenny rabbit and miss our pheasants! And what applies to rabbits, applies equally to other things. For my own part, I should never have dreamt of losing the esteem of my neighbours and getting into some desperate hobble on account of immorality. Others, I will not deny, may have been less particular.

To return to my story. I stayed at Southampton altogether six months. Then I came home. I had not been in Dulverton very long before a bobby knocked at the door with a summons—you know why. Accordingly, I had to appear at the justices' meeting, and, on the case being heard, received two months. When I got to Taunton, I found there was no fun or frolic as on the last occasion. We were locked up in separate cells, and left to repent of our sins in solitary confinement.

Curiously enough, on my release from prison, circumstances arose, quite independent of anything that had happened before, which brought me again to the neighbourhood of Southampton. It was the time of the Crimean War, and a man came home from the war, with whom I had formerly lived—" Larry " (or Harry) Oxenham. He acquired his nickname, like me, from a song, "Larry O'Brien." It appears that he and I got about drinking together, and I borrowed some money of him. Thereupon, just for a little fun, as if I had taken the Queen's shilling, he put the ribbons up in my hat. We went back to the Rock, got nearly tight, and Oxenham, pretending that he had enlisted me, filled in a form to that effect. We then joined the dancers—for it was Dulverton Fair—and in the midst of the excitement, he lost the paper. It was found by a man in the room, who, saying nothing to "Larry" or myself, was busy enough to take it to my mortal foe, Mr Bisset. Mr Bisset read the paper, and sent it off to the adjutant at Portsmouth. I ought to have mentioned that the man who "enlisted" me was a marine.

Confident that the whole thing was merely a joke, I thought nothing more about my "soldiering," and for a couple of months at least, matters remained quiet. Well, I was standing on Barle Bridge as I might now, when I saw a sergeant drive up through the town. It was not ten minutes before I saw him again — going down towards the house where I lived. He made inquiries, discovered that I was on the bridge, and told me his business. He began by asking whether I was an enlisted soldier.

"No," I said. "Larry and I had been drinking, and I had borrowed money of him."

"Oh, but," he replied, "it is on the paper that you enlisted, paid the fine, or smart money, twenty-one shillings, and that your brother and another were witnesses. The man you call Larry is now in the guard-room under arrest."

I stared.

"Well," continued the sergeant, "the upshot of the matter is that all three of you will have to go up to Portsmouth along with me."

The same evening we set off. We drove to
Tiverton, where the sergeant bought a bottle
of rum to drink on our journey up; and in
this and other ways, I am bound to say, he
behaved very well to us. After travelling half
the night, we arrived at Gosport, and from
Gosport we crossed a little arm of the sea to
Portsmouth. At Portsmouth the sergeant again
did us a friendly turn.

"Now," said he, "lodgings are dear here. If
you go to a lodging-house, you'll have to pay
a shilling a night each. But if you'll go down
to the barracks, to the receiving-room, you
can sleep there for nothing, and have a breakfast for sixpence apiece."

Of course, we agreed to that in a minute.
When breakfast-time came we were given a
good spread—bread and butter, and ham; and
everything was all right. Our thoughts then
turned to old "Larry," and we asked whether
we might see him during the morning. The
answer was, No; he was not to be seen. The
sergeant now ordered us to proceed to an
office to receive our pay. Somebody belonging
to the military concern planked down three-
and-sixpence, and similar payments were made
to us daily all the time we were there. The

I EXPERIENCE BAD LUCK

next thing we heard was that a colonel or
adjutant—one of those who were to try us—
was in the Isle of Wight, and would not return
for a week. To some this would have been
a vexatious delay, but, as we were being well
cared for, and none of us much given to worry,
we did not complain—in fact, we rather enjoyed
it.

At the week's end the call came. As we
were going along the street, we saw old " Larry "
between two soldiers, while a third marched
behind. We had, therefore, no opportunity of
speaking to him. One by one we were ushered
into the big room, while the others waited
outside. By-and-by my turn arrived, and I
was shown into a place where there were great
officers sitting all round the table. One of
them asked me questions.

" Is it true that you enlisted ? " he inquired.

" No, sir," I replied.

" Did you pay Oxenham any smart money ? "
he continued.

" No, sir," I answered. " 'Twas only a drinking spree, and I borrowed money of him. We
had lived together as servants." The others, it
appears, had said the same.

The officers looked to each other, and talked

for a little while, quietly among themselves. Then one of the head ones said,

" Aren't you in the habit of killing deer sometimes, and game ? " It was evident that he knew something about me, and about my ways.

"Yes," I said, " very often."

He smiled to the rest, and remarked, turning to me, " You can go."

After I came out, old " Larry " was released, and we went and had a spree together. The military authorities paid our fare home ; and, when we reached Dulverton, it happened that the bells were ringing. It sounded like a welcome, and everybody made out that it was in honour of "his lordship's" return.

In conclusion, I feel compelled to observe that the adjutant, or whoever it was that caused all this fuss, acted very stupidly. It was quite a common thing on fair days for a recruiting sergeant to stick the ribbons in a man's hat, who had no more intention of enlisting than the man in the moon. The whole thing was a plant, and the object was to induce young fellows to join, who had no means of paying smart money. But, of course, this object would have been defeated, if I, or any other chap who had been seen strutting about with the red, white,

I EXPERIENCE BAD LUCK

and blue, could not be excused from serving. The shortest way out of the difficulty was to pretend that we had paid the fine, though, as a matter of fact, we had paid nothing. I have sometimes wondered whether it was not a dodge of Mr Bisset's, to get rid of me. If so, I may flatter myself it was pretty much of a failure, as the only result was to give me a week's holiday at the expense of the Government.

This was one of those cases in which everything came right in the end, and justice, though tardy, at last befriended the innocent. It is not always so, and I could cite instances in which injustice has prevailed, assisted, it is to be feared, by lying and false swearing. Here is an example. I and another man called Nethercott went off to kill a pheasant—two, if we could manage it—on Squire Lucas's ground. At Stockham we saw some pheasants out to feed in a field—in the " urrishes," and round the ricks. I shot one, and Bill Nethercott went in and picked it up. A man outside at work descried my mate picking up the bird, and hastened down to find out who we were. We ran away. He, however, spotted us, and Nethercott and I were summoned. Now mark!

AUTOBIOGRAPHY OF A POACHER

When we came before the magistrates, the farmer's man swore positively that Nethercott both shot the pheasant and picked it up. As for me, for some reason or other, he would not swear to me at all. So it was I that committed the crime, and Nethercott that had to suffer. He got two months' imprisonment.

Perhaps this circumstance, that he bore my punishment, ought to have made me feel tenderly towards poor Bill, but, to be quite honest about it, he was more than a bit of a nuisance. I could hardly get rid of the man. He was always wanting to go about with me, and see me shoot. I may say that I was invariably the "forerunner" of all of them. My mates were very glad to stand by and witness the poaching, and help about the spoil, but very few of them carried guns. At last Tom Berry and I consulted together, and devised a remedy. We told Bill we had a receipt that would draw the rabbits for a mile around. He asked what it would come to, and we informed him two shillings. He was to get a big heavy stone, and we were to go with him to point out the kind of stone required. Meanwhile it would be necessary to buy certain stuff at the druggist's. Bill did not take much persuading.

I EXPERIENCE BAD LUCK

He handed over the florin, and we agreed to meet the following day.

At the time appointed we went down by a zigzag path to the bottom of Execleave, and reached a spot not far from Barlynch Abbey, where there is a fording-place. Here we searched about, and at length found a flat stone, which must have been a hundredweight or more. Making believe that we could not carry it, we got it up on the old man's back. Then we all began the ascent. The old man kept saying that the stone was terribly heavy, and every two or three minutes he was obliged to pause and rest. Sometimes he would ask us to help, but we always replied that we were not strong enough. It pleased him to be told how strong he was, and, hearing this, he would whip up again. At last he arrived with his burden at the head of the wood, where perhaps he thought to stop, but I would not let him.

"You must have a good heart," I said, "and not give out yet." So on he went, with the stone, to Heatheridge. The hill has now been taken into fields, enclosed, but at that time it was all common. Going, as near as we could judge, to the middle of the common, we took

the stone and laid it flat on the ground. I was
to pour the liquid on the middle of the stone,
while the others kept back, for fear they should
be caught sneezing. This ceremony was duly
carried out. The liquid in question was naphtha,
which I got, not from the druggist, but from
Joey Chidley, who drove the mail cart and used
it for singeing horses. On our way up from the
river, just to show what good stuff it was, I set
it on fire. Bill verily thought it a miracle, but,
for all that, he was not without his doubts. He
wanted to know how the rabbits would get
across the Exe. We answered they could not
help themselves, such was the power of the
stone.

After the anointing had taken place, we
stationed him where he could see the stone,
and cautioned him to remain very still.

" Keep your eye open," I said, "and you will
see flocks of rabbits come up. When they get
to the stone, they will smell at it, begin to
sneeze, and then dash out their brains. But
you are not to touch them till there is a cart-
load or more, all in a heap."

Having said this, we pretended to retire to a
convenient distance, but, in point of fact, went
home, leaving the old man in the middle of the

common, where he stayed all night in the cold.
It is needless to state that no rabbits came
across from Baron's Down.

When Nethercott came back he found his
way to our house and blew us up sky-high.
I didn't care for that. Then he cursed and
swore, and vowed he would never go out with
me again. I didn't care for that; in fact, I
did it for that very purpose. The story soon
became known, and for a long time afterwards
Nethercott did not dare to show his face in
the streets of Dulverton, as the boys kept
"tishing." However, when I recovered from
my drinking bout, I felt vexed for the old
fellow. Bread was dear in those days, and he
could not afford the two shillings.

Although my favourite modes of making
money would not, I suppose, be classed as
lawful, I was never against earning an honest
penny, especially if I could combine business
with pleasure. In the old days there was a
good deal of charcoal burning out in the woods,
and I recollect that an old man, called Robert
Johns, who had been brought up to coaling
from a boy, and was then burning for one Cox
of Southmolton, asked me to go with him.
I did not take long in answering, for I loved

the woods dearly. I could live out in the
woods. Well, I packed up my tools, my
trammel, and my gun, and wended my way
up Dulverton bottom to Shircombe Slade,
above New Invention, where Johns had a cabin
made of earth and grass. There I bestowed
my gun and net, while I set about my task,
which was dragging down the great poles for
Robert to cut up. I felt it hard work,
but stuck to my bargain, and then— But I
had better explain the sort of thing charcoal
burning is. First, you put a great pole in the
centre, and stack the timber all round. Then
you bury the whole stack with coal ashes—
culm, I think, is the proper name—pull out
the pole, put fire down the hole, and stop it
over, and the timber will smoulder for a couple
of nights and days.

After we had put fire to the first pit and
earthed it up and all, we went down to the
river fishing, caught a good lot, and, returning
to our cabin, cooked some of them. Amongst
our utensils were a crock, a frying-pan, a tea-
pot, and a plate or two, so that we were not
quite savages. Supper over, we retired to rest
in the cabin, lying down in the straw which
formed our bed. It was not usual for us to

take off our clothes. We fell into a dead sleep.
By-and-by old Rab Johns holloa'd out, and
I awoke. There was a great roaring like
thunder, and this it was that had aroused him.
The fact was that owing to our negligence—
we ought to have watched it every half-hour—
the pit was on fire! We threw what ashes
we had on it and fetched water from the river,
twenty yards distant, in our single bucket.
But it was not a bit of good; nothing could
stop the flames. The whole pit of coal, repre-
senting two or three waggon loads of wood, had
been spoilt, and the damage must have run
into pounds. Thought I to myself, "If that's
the beginning of coaling, I'm off." So I picked
up my tools and away to go, and had nothing
more to do with it. As for old Robert Johns,
he had to make the best of a bad job, and I
can assure you I didn't envy his interview with
Mr Cox after wasting so much of his precious
timber.

Few persons have consumed more liquor than
I have; still there was a time when—Heaven
knows for what reason—I either was or pretended to be a teetotaller. Temperance was
the fashion in some quarters then—principally
among the Dissenters—and I daresay it was

partly that, and partly a notion of bettering myself, that led me to join those people. Now I am a proper teetotaller, not having touched a drop of strong drink for several years. In those days I was a bit of a hypocrite. I used to go to chapel, and the chapel folks did not know but what I was a very strict abstainer. I sang in the gallery, and took tea at Mr Poole the minister's, who gave me and Ned the Sweep a house to pull down. A schoolroom was to be built on the site, and was duly erected, but the building has since been turned into houses, in one of which Mr German now lives. Just then a great teetotaller named Isaac Phillips came about. We became fast friends, and he used to take me with him when he went to lecture. What with listening to Mr Phillips's remarks, I came pretty near to being a lecturer myself. Outwardly, no doubt, I passed for a reformed character, but the fact is that ten minutes after I left Mr Phillips old mother would fetch my supper beer at the White Ball. At last, having gone out to a farmhouse, I got drunk, and some of them saw me rambling. This led to my expulsion.

I may as well give a few details about that farmhouse expedition. A certain farmer—he

I EXPERIENCE BAD LUCK

is dead now, poor fellow!—settled at a place called Ridler's. Guessing that I was a pretty good poacher, when harvest came he sent for me to help him. So, teetotaller as I was, or pretended to be, I carried out my nets and gun; and several from Dulverton besides me went out for the harvesting. Although I made out that I didn't drink, this farmer knew that I did all the time; so he used to bring me cold gin and water in a tea-pot, and the rest of the harvesters thought I was drinking cold tea. Well, after work was over for the day we went home, and then maister and I would set off night-hunting. The next morning when the harvesters arrived, they would find that maister was in bed, and then the following conversation would ensue:

"Where's maister then, missus?"

"Aw, he id'n a got up it. He id'n very well s' mornin."

"Where's Ocum? I don't zee nort o' ee."

"Aw, I s'pause he's up to slape—slapy-'eaded sort of fella."

She knew "the ropes" of it, and would tell them what to set about until we came down. After we were sufficiently rested we got up and went to work. When we carried the corn we had a jollification. Maister could play the fiddle, and so he supplied the music while we danced. A larking old chap, nice fellow though! When he took the jug to go down to draw cider, I used to step out at the back door, and, descending the cellar steps, drink a pint while he was drawing the liquor. That was my teetotalling—only a fancy or wish that people might think me an abstainer!

CHAPTER IV

I GO IN FOR BIG GAME

I⊤ must have been about this time that I left my mates and went in for something bigger. I don't like to say deer, though it was nothing else, from a fear that it may give some people a shock. We are all stag-hunters now, high and low, rich and poor ; and, if I were to shoot a stag to-morrow, I tremble to think what would become of me. Most likely it would be the same with me as with the niggers in America. "Hang him! Shoot him! Burn him!" would be the cry. Everybody in Dulverton would be down upon me, and I should pass the remnant of my days friendless and forlorn. This consideration leads me to repress a desire that sometimes comes over me—to shoot one more stag before I die, for in my time I have been a famous deer-killer, the greatest, I have heard it said, that ever flourished on Exmoor. This, however, is idle talk, since I am much too shaky to accomplish such a feat.

AUTOBIOGRAPHY OF A POACHER

A learned gentleman tells me that I belong to an ancient family, and that hundreds of years ago there were deer-killers at Dulverton. As you may not believe it, I will copy the paper he gave me, word for word.

"Dulverton, as a border manor of the Forest of Exmoor, is often mentioned in the perambulation accounts. The subject, a difficult one, may well be treated separately. In 1257 (42 Henry III.), Wm. Herelwyne and others killed a stag in the woods of Hawkridge, but William was not taken, for he could not be found. An inquiry followed which produced no result, whereupon the price of the stag was charged on four villages near. Hawkridge paid 4s.; Dulverton 5s.; Winsford, half a mark; and Withypool, 4s. In 1269, John de Regny de la Hele and others, with bows and arrows, killed a large hind (*bissam*) in the woods of Dulverton. John, too, did not appear, so the sheriff was ordered to distrain at his house, and produce him when wanted. In 1365, Robert Coram killed a stag in Dulverton, and was found hunting foxes in the forest; and Roger Dikelane and Walter Cromer killed a calf (*boviculum*) and a stag. Hugh Sydenham was on the jury in this case, as also in another in 1367, when James

I GO IN FOR BIG GAME

Dandiloc took a stag, and John Sully, Kt., took a staggart and a hind (*bissam*) in Easter week."

How about that for antiquity? But I don't propose to write a whole history of deer-poaching, going right back to the beginning of times, partly because I can't, and partly because, if I could, people would get weary of reading so many miles of print. I will, therefore, confine what I have to say merely to myself and my own experience. First, then, it is just to point out that I was grafted on to a period when there was either no stag-hunting at all in the neighbourhood, or the methods employed were ineffective, the result being that farmers were thrown on their own resources to protect their crops from injury. That I am not making this up anybody can see by looking into Dr Collyns's book. He always refers to deer-poachers, as if they were the biggest scoundrels unhung, but that does not lessen the value of his evidence. The contrary, I should say, though I am no lawyer. If I were, perhaps I should have got off oftener.

My second point is that, whether stags were being hunted or no, in my time and for people like me, the practice of shooting deer was neither unlawful, unsocial, nor uncivilised. I have read that in olden times all deer were the perquisites of the king, and anybody found killing them was liable to be hanged or mutilated. But when I was a young man, deer were not game at all, in the sense of being included in the Game Act. They were like rabbits—pensioners on the farmers; and their fate depended on the farmer on whose land they had taken up their quarters. If it was his aim to please the gentry, he would preserve them. If, on the other hand, he thought more of his wheat and his turnips than of other people's pleasure, he would send for his lordship of Dulverton, or, anyway, connive at what I did. When my old enemy, Mr Bisset, got into Parliament, one of his first moves was to obtain a law for the preservation of the red deer; and since then stalking them has been illegal, and attended with heavy penalties. Soon after this Bill was passed I remember seeing the following notice posted up in the streets of Dulverton!

I GO IN FOR BIG GAME

£5

REWARD.

WHEREAS

A STAG WAS SHOT

About a fortnight since, near Marsh Bridge, in Dulverton :

☞ The above Reward of FIVE POUNDS will be given by Mr C. P. Collyns, to any accomplice, or others, by whose evidence a conviction of the offender may be obtained. Any information leading to a conviction will be rewarded.

This, I believe, was the first official intimation that, from that time, deer-poaching must cease, or it would be the worse for the offenders. The announcement did not greatly interest me, as I had gone over, bag and baggage, to the other side. It was reported, however, that a cockney, born in Dulverton, offered six pounds for a stag, as a head was wanted for a Foresters' club-room. Dr Collyns had him up to his surgery, and the person implicated returned, it was said, to London two days before he intended. As the result of Mr Bisset's Act, deer-killing, except by the stag-hounds, had been entirely stopped in our part of the world. Some fellows up Porlock way tried it on a year or two ago, but the stag was taken from them, and they were fined to the tune of twenty pounds for destroying the deer, and another two pounds for carrying a gun without a licence. That reminds me that in my day, no gun licences were required, which was another reason why deer-killing was common. Such exemplary punishments make poaching of this sort unprofitable. In the case of a great animal like a stag, the risk of discovery is obvious ; and as nearly all the farmers go in for hunting, the poacher can expect no countenance from them. When I shot deer, their sympathies were, perhaps, evenly divided. They might not encourage their labourers, as this would endanger their relations with the landlord, but a regular professional of my standing was a different thing. They could trust him, and very often they did. I maintain, therefore, that my habits were not unsocial. Mr Bisset and his stag-hunters, of course, execrated me, but I was popular with my neighbours, if, indeed, I was not a hero amongst them. And that is what a man thinks of—not how those above him feel towards him, but how he is regarded by those of his own class with whom

I GO IN FOR BIG GAME

he naturally seeks friendships. Taking this as
a test, I venture to say that there was nobody
in Dulverton better liked or more highly
esteemed than myself. I will go even further
and assert that, amongst the gentry, those who
belonged to old Dulverton families and knew
me personally, never harboured an unkind wish
against me. They may have disliked my
poaching—no doubt, they did—but they did
not dislike me. Why should they? I was
always a very good sort of fellow.

If anybody had told me last week that I
should preach such a sermon as this, I shouldn't
have believed it. But, observing as I do the
change in public sentiment and the different
way these things are regarded nowadays, I
am anxious to justify myself to the younger
generation. As times are so altered I hardly
know whether it will be looked upon as a title
of honour or dishonour when I dub myself
"the last of the deer-killers." If, however, a
tombstone is erected to my memory, I should
choose these words as part of the inscription.
Having finished the preamble, I will now proceed to relate some of my experiences.

Perhaps the most famous poacher before
me was one Shapland of Northmolton, who

flourished about a hundred years ago. It is
related of him that one day he was out with
his father pursuing a hind, when he fancied
he saw the deer in the covert, and fired. As
it happened, it was his own father. The
wound did not prove mortal, but the shock
was too much for Shapland, and he never
again went out with his gun.

After this Northmolton man, I think no one
excelled in deer-killing more than my master,
Tom Bell. He was a middle-sized man, about
five foot seven or eight, and well-grown. If
I was a writer by profession, I believe I could
make out a pretty story about this Bell, as
he was only a labouring man and married a
farmer's daughter. I first got to know him
when I was a boy. Between the time when I
was hanged and joined the navvies at Starcross,
I worked for two years at Draydon, a farm on
the confines of wild moors; but as this was
a tame, unadventurous period of my life, I
passed it over in my opening chapter.

However, Bell was the farmer's son-in-law,
and he was a jolly fellow, up to all sorts of
larks with us boys, of whom there were two
or three in the house, one an apprentice. He
would put a slipping-knot in a long piece of

cord, tie it round my big toe, and, going back
to bed, pull so hard as nearly to twist my toe
off. I remember on one occasion he came
home and, finding me asleep, thrust the candle
he had "douted" into my mouth which was
all agape. Naturally, I shut my jaws when
he drew the wick through my teeth, leaving
the grease — a nasty, beastly mess — in my
mouth.

In spite of his roguery, we thought him a
capital fellow, a rare fellow—principally for
the following reason. After he had been talking with the old man and the old woman, he
would come out into the kitchen, where there
were assembled three or four servant men,
and we three boys. The maid also was no
doubt present, but he took no notice of her.
Removing his boots, he would pass in beside
the settle where the old man was sitting, and
go down into the cellar with a milking-pail.
He would let the cider run down by the side
of the pail, so as to avoid making a noise,
and, when the vessel was full, would bring it
upstairs, past the settle, and into the kitchen.
Men and boys, he would make us all partake,
and what was left, we carried up into the bedroom, and drank there. It chanced that one

night Bell went once too often. The old man allowed him to descend the stairs, and waited till he came up. He then stopped him with his pail. There was a bit of a bustle, and after that the door of the cellar was kept locked.

His father - in - law probably knew nothing about it, but we boys knew—wonder if we hadn't!—that Bell was a confirmed poacher. I recollect that he asked me to go out with him as a look-out boy. He caught a pheasant in a wire, and told me it was *an owl*. This was part of his craftiness. If I had known better, I should have come in partners and expected something. As it was, when he put the owl in his pocket, it seemed to me very funny. I am minded to tell you another anecdote, which will show you how artful he was. He was shooting one day on an adjoining farm, when somebody saw him. Perceiving this, he instantly ran home, took Tom the grey pony out of the stable, and off he rode, as fast as his horse could carry him, to Winsford. Arrived at the village, he walked into the Royal Oak, and said to the landlord,

"Mr Paull, do tell me what time it is. I want to know particular."

I GO IN FOR BIG GAME

Mr Paull told him the time, whereupon he had a pint to drink, mounted the pony, and rode home again. A day or two afterwards a summons was served on him for trespassing in pursuit of game. He appeared at the magistrates' meeting and called Mr Paull, who proved that, near about the time he was said to be poaching, he was at Winsford.

"How could he be poaching, when he was at my house?" asked the landlord, in astonishment. Case dismissed.

Well, after a while I left Draydon, where the diet was not to my mind. Every year they used to kill a bull, and the meat was so tough that it was not enough to bite it with your teeth. You had to tear at it with both hands. I had two basins of porridge a day, one for breakfast, the other for supper; and on Sunday mornings toast and cider, or whit-pot. Perpetual porridge did not agree with my constitution; no more did the hard monotonous life on a farm. So I sought my fortune on the railway, with what result you know. For a time I lost sight of Bell. When I next heard of him, he was at Dulverton. His father-in-law had given him a horse, and he was trying to earn a living as a carrier. Practically, however, he had come to nothing, and it became more and more a necessity with him to employ his talents in poaching, especially in deer-killing. This was in Captain West's and Mr Theobald's time. Both these gentlemen were foreigners, and had little idea of stag-hunting. In two months, Mr Theobald took only three deer, and his want of success was a great encouragement to Bell and others who came to the assistance of the farmers. At last the pack stumbled on a stag that Bell had hidden away, and which he accordingly lost. This, I believe, was his last stag, for soon after he went away to America, whither he wished me to accompany him, but I declined.

Before he left the country, Bell taught me his art. In the second of the mill hams at Dulverton there used to be a high elm—the largest tree in the neighbourhood. It stood in the hedge, and formed the butt at which we practised shooting. A little square piece of white paper was pinned to the stock, and when we could hit the paper, we were considered perfect. We rested the gun on a forked stick, and shot upwards. Guns were of all sorts in those days, and very few "threw" straight. I suppose Bell's reason for instructing me was

80

I GO IN FOR BIG GAME

that he wanted a partner, but I cannot remember that I ever went stalking with him.
In fact, I have never favoured company on
these occasions. Someone might tread on a
stick or say in a loud whisper, "Shoot straight
now!" and that would baffle me. My belief is
that I started in this way, and, as soon as I felt
myself competent, went out by myself. I
notice that Dr Collyns in one place speaks of
idle and lawless marauders — fustian-coated,
"early morning" looking gentry — who, in
order to secure the prize of a stag's head,
or horns, would "mortally wound" or "per-
manently injure" many deer. This may have
been true of bungling amateurs, such as farm-
servants, but is unjust to the professional
deer - killer, who was, generally speaking, a
dead-shot.

Now for the incident of my first stag. I
loaded my gun with a ball, and went off to
Execleave, where I stalked the woods. Just
as I was approaching Hele Bridge Wood, a
stag jumped up from his bed, and made me
a bit of a look. I thought he stood a worse
chance than I, shot at him, and the deer
came down. He had been hit on the back-
bone. The next moment he was dragging

himself down the hill, as steep as the roof of a house, towards the river. I followed, and seized him by one of the hind legs, but could not stop him. At last I got at his neck, whipped out my knife, and cut his windpipe. That finished him. I went home. The same night I hired a donkey and cart from Nethercott the rag-gatherer, returned with the carcass, and sold it out at sixpence a pound.

I thought this a fine job, as it turned in money, and that induced me to try again. I cannot fix the date of the occurrence, as it was so many years ago, but the event must have occurred in the summer. I can tell this because the stag had velvet on his horns, and stags lose their velvet in September. No surprise need be felt at the rag-gatherer's willingness to lend me his donkey. Scores would have helped in transporting a deer, as they knew they would be paid—two shillings. I may mention in confidence that no less than three different farmers, living in the parish of Dulverton, made me the offer of carting a carcass any time, but, of course, I must not betray their names.

In some of these remarks I have only stated the rules I generally followed, but I don't pretend to have been always consistent, or

I GO IN FOR BIG GAME

that my experiences were invariably alike. Thus the story I am about to relate may seem to contradict in some points what has been said before, but I can't help it if it does. Truth is truth, and lies are lies; and, so long as I stick to the one, and avoid the other, I shall not be concerned about seemings and appearings.

If you had entered our cottage one fine day, you would have seen two deer,—one young, and the other, as they say, warrantable—hung up by the heels. My story is about the former. A man came and told me that over in Burridge was a deer. This was hardly credible, as Burridge was a place to which deer did not resort in those days. However, I took his word, and cast about in my mind as to the best way of capturing the stranger. I knew a man who had a good dog, and sent him and another fellow to Northmoor—the house was not standing then—for the purpose of driving back the deer. Meanwhile I stationed myself in a shooting path, or an alley where they had been dragging timber. By-and-by I heard the dog bark, and the deer broke from the bushes close beside me. On seeing me, he turned and went up the wood. However, I shot at him, the ball entering his flank

83

and coming out at his neck. The deer dropped. The other two men, hearing the shot, hastened to the spot, and a consultation took place as to what was to be done with the deer.

"Carry him right home," was my proposal; but to this, as it was plain daylight, the others would not consent.

"Wait till night," said one of them.

"If you don't help carry him home," I said, "there's no money for you."

"I don't care," he replied; "I won't do it by daylight."

"Then," I answered, "you can go home."

So he crossed the water and went home to Lady Street.

Next I turned to the other. "Are you in the mind to help carry him?" I asked.

"Yes," he said, "I'll carry him as far as Blackwell's cottage." This was a little dairy just above Barle Bridge, and outside the town.

"Never mind," I replied; "I'll carry him up the street, if you'll catch hold of the head and keep the blood from coming against me."

So we carried home the deer to Duck Paddle (now Chapel Street), and hung him up with another that I had killed before. Things cannot be kept secret very long in a place like

84

I GO IN FOR BIG GAME

Dulverton, and soon tidings of my exploits reached the ears of two important gentlemen, old Dr Collyns and a Mr Gardner, who lived at the Green. They called to see the deer. Hardly had they entered the cottage when my mother was in a brave way.

"Don't show them," she holloa'd down to me, "or they'll take them away."

"I'll see they don't do that," I answered. As a matter of fact, they were parcelled out and sold. This incident proves that I was a proper poacher, and not afraid of anybody. On another occasion I did a still more daring thing. It was a hunting morning, and I met with a couple of sporting characters, who called me into the Lamb, and said,

"We'll give you half-a-crown, and plenty of brandy and water, if you'll take a haunch up to the Red Lion corner, and stand there till the hunters come out."

It was no small risk, but I agreed, drank up my liquor, received my half-crown, and started. The first to appear was Squire Locke. I had the haunch on my back, across my shoulder, and catching hold of the head of his horse, I asked,

"How would you like to whit up your chops on that this morning?"

"Oh, you rogue!" he cried.

"No rogue at all," I made answer. "I shot my deer out of the way, and didn't run him to death with hounds."

We had all sorts of rows. Amongst other things he asked me what I would do.

"Nothing," I replied, "in the shape of work."

He and I stayed jawing for the best part of half-an-hour, while some of the field stood by and listened. Then I went home. I have often thought that this was the narrowest escape from a horse-whipping I ever experienced. I cannot quite account for it, but perhaps my boldness mesmerised them.

Not long after a man of Exford sent for me. He did not state his business, but I guessed what it was. I took my gun and set out very early in the morning for his house, some ten or twelve miles away. We had dinner, and got strolling over the Exmoor hills in search of a deer. Not a deer could we see till we came to Badgeworthy. By-and-by we marked one coming in over the hill, waited and stalked, and got within shot of her—it was a hind. She proved to be big with calf, and we opened her. This done, we buried her over, hiding her away with heather till night. When we came to fetch her, we found that a dog or foxes had eaten a lot of her, and spoilt one of her haunches. However, we took her home to his house, skinned her, and made the best of her. I claimed as my share the haunch—the good one, I mean.

" Is that all you're going to have ? " asked my mate.

" Quite enough for me to carry to Dulverton from Exford," I replied. So I brought it home, and carried it down through the streets of the town on the top of my gun. It happened that I reached Dulverton just as the men were going to work, and they greeted me with shouts— " Here comes my lord with another deer ! "

The Dulverton men composed a song about my carrying deer through the town. Most of the verses I have forgotten, but one was as follows :—

How you would have laughed to see limping Jack,
As he trudged along with a buck on his back,
Just like an old Irishman carrying his pack,
    Right fol the dol little o lido.

I am not lame, but a heavy deer is a considerable load, enough to make any one stagger.

I said a little way back that I never went out stalking with Tom Bell, and I never did *as a disciple.* I recollect, however, a job in which three of us took part—Tom Bell, Tom Berry, and his lordship, myself. Accompanied by a dog, we set off for Haddon Hill to try for a deer. We stayed hunting about for several hours, and were not successful. At last a heath-poult rose, and putting the gun to my shoulder, I aimed at the bird.

"Ah!" said I to my mates, "if only the gun were loaded with shot, how easily I could have killed it!"

All these moves, it seems, were being watched by Lord Carnarvon's men, five or six in number, and when I put the gun to my shoulder, it happened that they were quite close. Amongst them was the old deer-harbourer, Jem Blackmore. Coming out from the bushes, they cried,

"We've got you, haven't we?"

"Got us about what?" I asked.

"Oh, you were pointing with your gun at that poult," was the reply.

"Well," said I, "if I was pointing at it, I didn't shoot."

However, it was the old story. Mr Bisset, who rented the shooting over the manor, soon knew it, and once more I was summoned for trespass in pursuit of game. Berry and I were sentenced to two months' imprisonment; but Bell gave them the slip, and neither Berry nor myself split on him. By this time I had gone to jail so often that, at last, it became a joke. The turnkey, on seeing me, used to laugh, and say,

"You've come again then, Holcombe?"

"Too true," I would answer, and laugh with him.

But I have had some hair-breadth escapes, too. Here are some of them.

One day, taking my trammel, I went up to Tarr Steps, with another man, to try my luck in a little fishing. On the edge of the evening —fish sometimes sport like fun in "the dimpse" —I had made a start by spreading my trammel, when my companion sang out,

"Mr Jekyll and his man are coming!"

He recognised the individual by the black clothes he was wearing. Mr Jekyll was a parson. I pulled in my trammel pole, drew in as close to the bank as I could, myself, and in that position heard them pass. They were quite near, and could have touched me with a stick. Keeping their eye on the water, they proceeded some distance upstream, after which, I suppose, they concluded that they had overshot the mark.

At all events, my mate, who was on the other side of the water, shouted to me,

" They're coming back again."

I made a dash across the river, and my mate and I scampered up over the woods of Ashway Hat as hard as ever we could go. I imagine they couldn't face the water; we, at least, saw no more of them. I had been pretty rash in entering the water on Mr Jekyll's side, for just opposite—separated from the river by a big meadow, like a lawn—was his house, from which he could look right down on my actions.

Not at all discouraged by the result of this adventure, we went up to Ashway Farm, and down across some fields to Three Waters, where we began again. Thence we fished all down the river to Dulverton, and when we reached the town, we had a nice load.

The manservant afterwards took a public-house at Battleton, called the " Country House," and I used to tease him about the affair. He made out then that he had no wish to catch us. His story was, that he saw us plainly enough, and advised his master to go further up the stream. I can hardly believe it.

I have had two or three other " close shaves," which it may interest the reader to hear of.

I GO IN FOR BIG GAME

Execleave was formerly the property of Mr Richard Beague, who employed an old man called Brewer to look after the woods for him. One day I was strolling through the coverts in search of game, when I saw a hare sitting. I immediately took my gun out of my pocket, and putting it together, shot the hare. No sooner had I picked her up, than I saw the old man coming along one of the shooting paths. He was so close that it was impossible for me to run away, but there were a number of big trees then, as there are now—doubtless the same—and I chose out a fine great oak to hide behind.

As the old man came on, I dodged round this tree, carefully regulating my movements so as to be exactly opposite him, and holding the gun in front of me. All this time the hairs of my head were, so to speak, heaving up in my hat. Having circumnavigated the tree, I waited till the old man was out of sight, and then, wasn't I glad? I took off the leather that kept the barrel and stock together, and soon skedaddled out of the way. I might, of course, have run away before, had I liked, nor, at his time of life, could he have given chase. But he was near enough to have been able to swear to me, and I think, therefore, I followed the wiser course.

On another occasion I was on Winsford Hill, walking the heath and trying for a poult, or blackcock. One rose, and I killed him. At the same moment I saw a man on a pony coming round the bend of the hill. I fell right down on my belly in the heath, and could not lift my head, or he would have seen me. I had to depend on guessing. After a while I thought he must have gone by, and raised my head just in time to discover who it was—viz. old John Rawle that looked after the ponies. Poor old fellow, he had passed without seeing me. He had warned me several times before, and, though a good old man, I think he would have told now, as he had said,

" This is the last time I shall overlook it."

However, all's well that ends well. I was glad to rise, put my gun in my pocket, and away to go. One more slice of luck.

A gentleman once came to me, saying that he wanted a bird particularly, to send away. Accordingly I took my gun, went off, searched all over Heatheridge, and could see nothing. I adjourned to Stockham, looked into two or three stubble fields thereabouts, and still I could see nothing. I continued my search past Stockham House and down to Stockham Park —a field through which there is a footpath leading to Chilley Bridge. I looked into this field, in which corn had been recently cut, and in the middle I saw a cock-pheasant.

So far, so good. The case, however, presented some difficulty, as the keeper lived in a cottage just below, and well in sight. I began to consider how I should have that bird, but— well, it was a poser. However, keeper or no keeper, I thought to myself, I must have it. So I took the gun out of my pocket, divested myself of my coat, turned it inside out, and did the same to the hat—a billycock. This, of course, was intended as a means of disguise. I went into the woodside, stalked down, peeped through the hedge, and saw that the bird was busy feeding. When he had had his fill, he began to draw back towards the covert—in other words, towards me. When he came within easy distance, and I thought I could kill him properly, without causing him to flutter about, I shot him, went in, and picked him up.

As I did so, I heard the garden gate fall, and, looking down to the cottage, saw Jim Hobbs, Squire Lucas's keeper, coming up. However, that didn't frighten me. Although I had the bird in one hand, and my gun in the other, which gave the keeper an advantage, still I was young and "flippant," not used to work, and I felt sure that he couldn't catch me. The only danger—it was not a serious danger, perhaps—was, that he might recognise me. Away I went up to the gate, and out in the road, along which I ran a short distance to make him believe that I had taken that route. Instead of that I clambered over the hedge, and passed up through the wood.

When I reached what I considered a point of safety, I was very glad to stop ; after running so far, I wanted a new pair of bellows. I never saw any more of Mr Hobbs, nor did I hear any more about the affair. On arriving home I told the gentleman what I had been through, and naturally he was much interested. I forget what he paid for the bird, but I recollect that he treated me well, and gave me something extra.

I can relate a still more striking adventure, or rather string of adventures, out of which I had the good fortune to escape scot free. In those days there lived at Comer's Cot, under Sir Thomas, an old woodman called Chilcot—

I GO IN FOR BIG GAME

a faithful retainer, I suppose, he would have been called, but that was nothing to us. Not far from Comer's Cot is Red Cleave, a noted plantation then of larch firs, in which you can see pheasants better than in black firs. Most of the trees have since been felled. Comer's Cot and Red Cleave are both by the Exe, a few miles upstream from Dulverton, but I need not indicate the locality, as it must be known to most people owing to the stag-hunting.

Well, the first time I ever went up there poaching, having entered the covert, we found a bird, had a shot at it, and killed it. Almost at the same moment we heard a weird sound proceeding, as it seemed, from the bedroom window of the cottage, which we afterwards learnt was caused by a bullock's horn. That frightened us. Off we started without staying to have more than that one shot, and resumed operations in another place, and at a secure distance.

However, a few nights later, we thought we would try again, and see if the strange noise was repeated. We went, had a shot, and no sooner was the shot fired than the old horn began to blow again. So we said to each other that we had better beat a retreat. By this time we had come to be intensely interested in that horn, which exercised a sort of fascination over us. Once more we visited Red Cleave, had a shot, and again the horn began to blow. Thereupon we consulted together and decided that, as long as the horn continued blowing down there, we would keep shooting. Accordingly, we went on helping the horn. We shot four or five birds that night, and each time came the music of the horn, which had no longer any terrors for us. In fact, we had got delighted with it, and deemed ourselves safer with the horn than without it.

The next time I went out, I had a new mate, and I thought it only fair to warn him that in one of the places I was going to, we were likely to hear some music, "but," said I, "you have no occasion to be frightened."

"All right!" he answered.

We went up in the wood, and seeing what I thought was a pheasant, I shot at it. Down it came, when it turned out to be nothing but an old magpie. Swollen up in "frisky" weather, a magpie looks very much like a hen-pheasant. We kicked the bird on one side, and then I said to my mate:

"Why, how's this? There's no music after shooting."

I GO IN FOR BIG GAME

We advanced a few steps, found another bird, shot it,—and then no lack of music! We heard the bushes cracking, and saw faces peering—lots of them. Away we bolted to the thickest place we could find, and thence to the hedge. I may observe parenthetically that a poacher never makes for a gateway if he can help it, as that is the place where they try to nab you. Through the hedge I broke, the bushes swinging back against my face; but it is better to have bushes knocking you in the face, than three months in prison. Then we ran for our lives. Probably they mistook our direction, for we saw no more of them. His lordship got clear again.

If I were a proper story-teller, I should entitle my next tale, "Unbuttoning a Sheep's Collar." You don't know what that means now, but you will directly. One day I was asked by a poor man living in a cottage, with no land of his own, to go night-hunting. Knowing that I was accustomed to do a good deal of poaching, he invited me to stay a week or a fortnight. Accordingly, I went, and took a friend. There were plenty of hares round there, and on the first night we had pretty good sport. When we came back in the morning, my mate observed that he smelt meat, but at the time we took no further notice of the circumstance.

All three went to bed. Our host, the labourer, had to go to work at seven o'clock, but, as we poachers were not under this necessity, we lay on. The wife brought us some breakfast, and afterwards some dinner. I should state that the cottage stood in a very solitary spot, with no houses near; otherwise we could not have managed as we did.

The man returned about four or five; and when it began to grow dark we got up, had supper, smoked a pipe, and held a discussion as to the best coverts to visit. About eight o'clock we sallied forth, and again met with a pretty good night's sport. We came home, went to bed, and were struck—this time more than before—with the pervading smell of meat. We decided to use flint and steel and strike a light. We got out, drew a match from a bundle—one of the extraordinary matches then in use, with great dobs of brimstone as big as horse beans, or at least peas, on each end —and having lighted a candle, commenced searching about. At last we found the meat, sure enough, and pretty much of it too. It was my mate who discovered it.

"Come here," he said—he didn't speak loud —"here's meat ; come over and see."

I crossed the room, and there I saw a barrel half full of something salted in. Whereupon I remarked :

"This won't do, you know. This is mutton, sheep's collar unbuttoned. They'll be searching the house—that'll be the next thing. I shan't stay here." (I felt certain that the man hadn't bought the meat. He only got seven shillings a week.) "I shall be off."

"We may as well stay one night more," answered my mate ; "we've had good sport."

"Just as you please," I said, "but I don't like the appearance of it."

Accordingly, the following night we went out again, and again enjoyed very good sport. We had passed no remarks either to the man or his wife as to the barrel and its contents, but as I did not relish the idea of seven years' transportation, I said on our way back :

"We are thinking that it's time we went home. If we stay about too long, we may get caught."

"All right!" he replied.

AUTOBIOGRAPHY OF A POACHER

We returned to the cottage, lit the fire, and had a cup of tea and some breakfast. After that we shared our money, or at least paid him off, and having picked up the "ragged shirts" (or nets) prepared to carry home the hares, accompanied by our faithful dog. On taking leave we wished him good - morning, and promised to come again some day. But we never went again; sheep-stealing was not exactly our line.

Most people regard a poacher's as a lawless sort of life, and one likely, as the good chaplain warned me, to lead a man into trouble. But a regular calling is not without its dangers, and certainly my own attempts to gain a living otherwise than by my gun have been peculiarly discouraging. It will be readily understood that occasionally Dulverton became too warm for me, and, finding that I could not go out without being watched, I was glad to migrate for a time to some other place. Once I took it into my head that I would go up the country. No trains ran here then, so I walked into Tiverton, and took a ticket for Bath. I had plenty of money in my pocket, and on reaching my destination, secured lodgings for the night. The next day I travelled about the streets in search of a job, but saw no work that would suit me. However, the day after I set out again with the same intention, and entered a yard, where there were six pairs of sawyers. Everything in those days was sawn by hand. I was not a professional, but I had been used to a little sawing at Tom Zadley's, so I asked if there was any chance for a pit-sawyer.

"Yes," was the reply, "chap's just gone."

I resolved to do my best, and for several weeks I got on very well and earned good money. I felt it hard work, however — any work would have been hard then; I wanted my own fling—and that was not the worst. All those old sawyers, I found, were extremely fond of beer, nor was I very short. So one day we got tossing for beer. We tossed, and tossed, and tossed, until we grew drunk there in the yard. Then one of the chaps fell out with me, and we came to blows. He got my thumb in his mouth and nearly bit it off. At length they pulled him away, and my thumb was released. I put sticking plaster on my injured member, and tied it up; but, after that, I did not care to remain in the place. By this time I had become a pretty good professional with a saw, and thought I could get work anywhere. As I knew several Dulverton men at Bristol, I went to see them. They informed me where the saw-yards were, and after a while I got another job. I did not take long, however, to discover that things were forty times worse there than at Bath. Drink—talk about drink! It was *nothing but beer.* Earn what you might, it all went in liquor, and you were bound to do as others did. I had got into very rough company, and, realising this, was afraid to stay with them. Unless you followed your neighbour, they thought nothing of you, you were nobody ; and, as some of them were Irish fellows, there were continual brawls. At length I came to feel that if I remained much longer with that crew, I should stand an excellent chance of being transported or killed ; whereas, if I was caught poaching, the utmost that I need fear was three months' imprisonment. Better that than penal servitude, for hard work I didn't care for. Accordingly, I went home.

I may here mention one or two minor adventures, which seem to me rather singular. One day my father and I were out night-hunting, when it began to rain heavily. For shelter we got into a linhay at Red Cross, King's Bromp-

ton, and, supposing that we were alone, talked
about the game we had caught and where we
were going. We had not been there long,
however, before I fancied I heard someone
fetching breath. I scraped about, and presently
found my hand on a man's face in the crib.
I was rather frightened, certainly, but my fears
proved groundless. The men — there were
three of them in all—turned out to be of the
same profession as ourselves; in fact, we knew
them. After a time the rain cleared, when
they went their way, and we ours. I suppose
the fellows lay still in order that they might
hear our business.

On another occasion my brother Willie and
myself were shooting in Brushford parish,
when we observed somebody climbing a steep
field towards us. It was darkish, and neither
of us had the least doubt but that the man
was a keeper, otherwise he would not have
been so bold as to interfere with poachers at
their work. By-and-by he reached the top,
opened the gate, and came out into the lane.

"What be doing here?" he asked.

For answer, Willie knocked him down. The
next day it was reported that So-and-So had
been terribly assaulted by the poachers. Now

AUTOBIOGRAPHY OF A POACHER

So-and-So was what we term a mazed man—
at any rate, he was half-witted—and this,
though we had not the least idea who or what
he was, made our conduct appear shameful.
Needless to say, we avoided that place for
some time.

CHAPTER V

HOW DR COLLYNS AND I GOT ON TOGETHER, AND MORE ABOUT DEER

IN the course of my story I have several times mentioned the name of Dr Collyns, and as he was one of my chief opponents, I think it well to write a chapter about our conflicts. I shall give him his character presently. Meanwhile, I may explain that he was the man who set the Devon and Somerset pack of stag-hounds on its legs, and I suppose there never was a more eager and skilful stag-hunter. So, of course, he and I were what you call natural enemies, and, living in the same place, could not help coming in contact with each other. Dr Collyns was a very stout gentleman.

Now for a little deer-killing. Going off with my gun to Execleave, I stalked the woods, and seeing a deer, shot at him. I perceived I had knocked him hard, and followed him up so as to keep him in sight. Sometimes the deer would lie down, and then, when I came over-near to him, would rise up and start off again. I had no more powder, as my mate, in whose hands it was, had gone home, having lost me. At last the deer took to the water. Fearing that he might enter Lord Carnarvon's grounds, where there were keepers, I got in front and turned him. Sometimes he would come out into the wood, and, to cut matters short, I kept following that deer up and down from ten in the morning till four o'clock in the afternoon. Then he left the water, crossed over under Barlynch wall, and lay down.

Without knowing whether he was alive or dead, I gave up the pursuit, and ran home to re-load my gun. I found my mate in the shop with my father, loaded my gun, and set off again. Tucking up my trousers, I forded the river and approached the place where I had last seen the deer. He was still there. I shot him again, but there was no need. He was dead—in fact, he had been dead all the time, and was now almost cold. I hid him away with ferns and such rubbish as was about, and, when night came, fetched him with a cart. Having brought him home, I sold out the carcass—what I could sell, and the rest I took to Bampton.

HOW DR COLLYNS AND I GOT ON

The next day I went about drinking, and, before the old doctor's door, began throwing about my money. The old doctor came out and interfered. He told me I ought not to do it. At length he interfered so much that he and I got to loggerheads, and I took off my jacket to fight with him. Well, he certainly was not going to fight with me, and, as he refused, I beat him with my jacket into the house. No gentleman would put up with such behaviour as that, so I was not surprised when Dr Collyns sent the constables after me to have me locked up. I was taken into the Red Lion, and kept there two or three days. At the end of that time I thought I would have a bit of fun with the constables. I made a bolt for it, cleared my way through the midst of them, ran down Chapel Street, through Ned the Sweep's house, and lay down in my father's garden between the beans. The constables followed in pursuit, and mother told them where I was. You may think this strange, but the truth is that the old soul was never better pleased than when I was in prison. She knew then that I was safe. I was tried and sent to jail for a month.

It so happened that the head turnkey had

come to Dulverton with an Exmoor murderer, for the purpose of bringing him before the magistrates; and we had given him fish. He now requited this kindness by taking me off the wheel, and putting me to work in the garden. He also cleaned out the debtor's ward for my accommodation, supplied me with a little extra grub, and even found me in 'baccy. So, you see, there's nothing like having friends at court.

This was not the only occasion on which I went through a performance outside Dr Collyns's door. But I ought to say something about my jacket. It was of velvet, and on the buttons were raised figures of hounds, foxes, and stags. The most important items, however, were the large pockets in which I carried a small gun in two parts. This story is so like the last that I hardly know whether it is worth relating, but you shall be the judge of that. I had gone into one of the woods—Ball Neck, I believe—knowing that a very fine stag was in lair, and the stag was shot. As soon as I had covered him with leaves and bushes, I returned to Dulverton, and paid my respects to a man of the place who kept a horse and kerry. But perhaps you never heard of a kerry. It is a

HOW DR COLLYNS AND I GOT ON

long cart with rails for sides, and used for conveying wood and turf. We were not long in arranging terms. Accordingly, when it was dark, the deer was taken up, placed in the kerry, and driven to Exeter, where he was sold. The money received for him was spent at Dulverton in a jollification. After we had been drinking for some time, an incident took place, intended to cause merriment, but one which might have ended seriously. Knowing Mr C. P. Collyns's likes and dislikes, and his great indignation when anyone killed a deer, I stationed myself outside his house, and shouted,

" Hark for'ard, hark for'ard,
Tantivy.
The stag was shot yesterday, and we are having a jolly
spree to-day."

Dr Collyns came to the surgery door, and sent for a parish constable named Saunders. He answered the summons and confronted me with his staff, while Dr Collyns exclaimed in a towering rage,

"Saunders, knock that man down like a bullock!"

Thereupon I took off my velvet jacket, and would have struck the constable, had not a

109

venerable old lady stepped between us, and pacified me. It was my aged mother.

My next story is rather different. One afternoon Tom Berry and myself went off poaching. We had got as far as Heatheridge, when whom should we meet but old Dr Collyns.

"How far are you fellows going, then?" he asked.

"I can't say," I replied, "but we mean to try and earn a shilling or two."

"Poaching again, I suppose?" he remarked.

"Yes, I suppose, doctor," I answered.

"Oh, well," he said, "I am going with you."

"Well!" said I, "I can't kill anything, if you keep riding alongside me."

"Exactly," he replied, "that is my object."

We would rather have had his room than his company. However, we took no further notice and pursued our way over Heatheridge and Court Down, keeping to the road so as to avoid an action for trespass. Meanwhile we chatted away to each other, just as if no third person were present. Finding that we could not get rid of him, we asked him if he would lend us a few shillings.

"Pretty fellows to lend money to," he replied. "I wonder whenever I should see it again."

HOW DR COLLYNS AND I GOT ON

"Well," said I, "I'll tell you what, doctor. I've got a fishing-net at home, if you would please lend me some money on it."

"Ah!" he answered, "bring it up at such and such a time."

The gentry were terribly opposed to fishing-nets, and would buy them up. So they would poachers' dogs, and kill them. It happened that I had an old net that was worn out, used up, and good for nothing. This article, at the time appointed, I carried up to the surgery.

"How much money d'ye want?" inquired the doctor. That was the way he used to speak—short, sharp.

"Eight shillings, please, sir," I answered.

He put his hand in his pocket, drew out eight shillings, and gave them to me. I thought myself a fine fellow.

"You have brought me your net," he said, "and it will remain in my possession until you fetch it and repay the loan. When will that be?"

"I don't know," was my reply. As a matter of fact, I never fetched it, but Dr Collyns did not trouble, as he thought the want of my net would keep me from fishing. But there may possibly have been another explanation. Dr Collyns was a very good, liberal, kind-hearted

III

gentleman, and I believe if he had known me to be destitute, he would readily have given me a few shillings. He had lent my father pounds. If poor people needed boots, he would advance them money to buy them with. I cannot run him down. He was a thorough good old English gentleman.

It may be worth adding that this was not the only time we were followed and thus baulked of our sport. Between Barle Bridge and Battleton, beside the river, runs a path called Pound Lane, almost parallel with the main road, which it joins at those points. Well, one evening my father and I went out for the purpose of night-hunting. We had crossed Barle Bridge, and passed into "the pound," when all at once we met the young Peppins. The young fellows must have noticed our dog, for, on looking back, we observed they were following us. We endeavoured to shake them off by circling. Out of "the pound," back by the road to Dulverton, into "the pound," back by the road — that was the dodge, but the Peppins were used to hare-hunting and circled after us. So it went on till one or two o'clock in the morning, when we went home. What was the strangest part of the business, during all this time we spoke never a word to them, nor they to us. The father of the young gentlemen, Mr George Hall Peppin, of Old Shute, was a friend of Dr Collyns, and assisted him in forming the Devon and Somerset pack of stag-hounds.

I have now done with Dr Collyns, but not with his house. Not that I was guilty of house-breaking, for, as you have been already informed, I did not stoop to rogueries of the sort —but you shall hear. I was very hard up, pretty nearly nonplussed, when somebody told me that up at Dr Collyns's, thrown on a dung-hill or dust-heap, was an old pheasant. I stole round to the spot, and picked it up. On examining it, I came to the conclusion that it was a tame bird which most probably had died a natural death. At any rate, all the flesh was gone, and nothing was left but the feathers. At first I hardly knew how to proceed about selling it, but, having met with a Dulverton man, I took his advice and split back the breast. Now the problem was what to put in so as to fill up the inside of the pheasant, and make it heavy. It so happened that at Yerd's Barn—on the site of the pretty house where Mr Giles lives—a pack of harriers was kept, Mr Peppin's, in fact;

and the huntsman's name was Roach. I knew
Roach well, and from him I obtained a leg of
carrion—in other words, of a horse.

I took out my knife, cut out some beautiful
slices, and carried them home, where I clapped
them into each side of the breast, and into the
belly, of the bird, very neatly. We then procured a needle and thread, and sewed up the
rent, which could not be seen. Having prepared
the pheasant for the market, we requested my
mother to sell it. We asked her, however, not to
dispose of it in the town, but carry it up to Joe
Chidley, the mail-cart man, whose duty it was to
drive every day to Tiverton. The old lady was
quite unsuspicious and never dreamt but that it
was fresh killed, so, without demur, she went and
sold the bird, and made two shillings of it.

After a while, however, she smelt a rat. We
were always laughing about that old pheasant,
and by-and-by she found out the secret. She
was in a dreadful way, and declared she would
sell no more game for us. She did not long
remain in this state of mind. From time to
time she got a tip from gentlemen, and, in her
situation, the temptation was irresistible. It
may not be believed, but is true nevertheless,
that in those days I sold plenty of game and

HOW DR COLLYNS AND I GOT ON

venison to gentry, many of them professed
hunters, and some of them with nearly as high
a title as my own.   For, please, do not forget,
I am Lord Mansfield.

I am supposed in this chapter to be writing
about deer, but deer and hares and pheasants
get sometimes mixed up.   Here is a case in
point.   A farmer at Haddon sent word to me
to come up and kill the deer.   They were eating
his turnips so.   At that time there existed no
deer-damage fund, and less heed was paid to
such conduct than would be the case now.   In
the present day, if a farmer engaged a deer-
killer, there is little doubt he would receive
notice to quit.   However, I went up on two or
three nights, but, as I could see no deer, got
tired and threw up the job.   One night, as I
was returning home, I saw a pheasant on a tree.
Thinking to ascertain whether my poor old gun
would carry straight enough to kill it, I shot at
it with a ball.   I was lucky; the bird dropped
dead.   Another time I was out with an old
one-legged blacksmith, who lived "out over" in
Anstey parish, and was a receiver of deer.   We
could find nothing of that sort about, but, looking over the hedge, my companion espied a
hare at the bottom of a field.

"Jack!" he cried, "do let us have your gun to see whether I can kill her."

He rested his gun on the hedge, fired, and killed the hare with a ball. As a rule I was my own receiver, but once, I recollect, a man of Dulverton bought a stag of me outright. He was a fine chap, a bugler in the Yeomanry, and I rather fancy I have mentioned him before. Having skinned the deer and cut off the feet, he conveyed the rest of the carcass to Bristol. Unfortunately, his customers did not know whether they were buying a deer or a donkey, and I was given to understand he made a very poor bargain. Anyhow, he did not trouble me for any more venison.

Strange to say, there were people at Dulverton who talked as if *I* did not know the difference between a donkey and a deer with his jacket on,—I who knew more about deer than, perhaps, any man then living, with the exception of old Jem Blackmore, the harbourer. It was on this wise. There dwelt at Dulverton for many years an Italian rag and bone collector. I am not sure that it was his right name, but we, at any rate, called him John Consenna. This Consenna had a donkey which was allowed to run about and pick up his food

HOW DR COLLYNS AND I GOT ON

in Execleave. One morning the donkey was found dead with a ball through him, and, most unfairly, I was accused of shooting him. I was much too clever to make a mistake; and, as to doing it maliciously, John and I had played cards many a night together, and I would never have hurt a poor man.

Of course, I was in some quarters a well-hated and very unpopular character; and not only I, but all who were suspected of encouraging me, had to suffer in consequence. I propose to give illustrations of this. One day I set out for Hawkridge bottom, where was a piece of young grass to which, I knew, the deer used to resort. I had not been in the wood very long before I saw a fine stag coming towards me with the evident intention of feeding in that plot. My gun was ready loaded with three balls. On came the deer till he was right opposite me. Even then he neither smelt nor saw me. It was most curious. I shot him. After he had been shot he staggered a few steps in my direction and fell over a high rock, close beside me. When I came to look, I found that his legs were broken and he had knocked himself terribly. It is probable that he would have died in any case, as he had the

bullets in him, but as often as not you don't
see them drop unless you follow them. I took
out his inside and concealed the deer with
leaves. Then, as I was quite alone and could
do no more, I went home. I told my father
what had happened, and as soon as it was late
enough, he and I and another man set out to
fetch him. We could not have done with fewer,
as, in our language, the stag was a proper
" belliser." We arrived at the spot, found the
deer all right, and, having tied his four legs
together, hoisted him up on a long pole. This
done, we started for Dulverton, and, taking it
by turns, carried him two at a time, one before
and another behind. Hynam Hill is steep, and
it was only by very hard work that we got the
deer home. At length, however, our efforts
were rewarded, and we deposited our spoil at
Duck Paddle.

The next day I went out to see about selling
it, and a shopkeeper in Fore Street, hearing
that I had some venison, came to me and
asked me to spare him the head and the skin.
I assented, and made a good price of the
articles. It appears that news of the trans-
action reached the ears of the gentry, and, as
he had dealings with such a notorious poacher,

HOW DR COLLYNS AND I GOT ON

my friend lost a lot of custom. That, of course, was no concern of mine, and I found quite sufficient occupation in disposing of the remainder.

As regards myself, my unwavering attitude was one of defiance. I referred just now to Hynam Hill. At the foot of this hill is Castle Bridge, so named, I suppose, after Mouncey Castle, though there is no proper castle that I ever saw—only earthworks. Close to Castle Bridge stands a large beech, and on this beech I used to carve stags, knowing that the hunters would pass that way and observe them. The idea occurred to me one day when I was up there fishing, and my object was to "terrify" them. That there might be no mistake, I spitted out a mark near each stag's heart to show the place of the bullet. I may. mention that I have killed at least three deer in the neighbouring wood, which is rather appropriately called Buckminster. The stags pretty artfully carved with their horns, brow, bay, and trey, and perhaps two or three on top, might still be seen a few years ago, but I am not sure they are there now. If you were passing that way, you might look round, and come back and tell me.

I will give you another instance of my "effrontery." There happened to be a meet of the stag-hounds, and I thought I would go for a day's hunting with them, partly for enjoyment, and partly with the idea that I might get into closer touch with the master, Mr Bisset. So away we went to Bury Hill, found the deer on Haddon, drove him to Bittiscombe, and out to the fish-ponds at Withiel Florey. There we waited. It was not unusual to wait for hours in one place, as we knew from experience that the deer would very probably come back.

So it fell out on this occasion. The deer returned, and was killed just above Clammer. We foot people ran down through the wood, hoping to be in at the death. When we arrived, the deer was in the water, and the huntsman and others were in the act of pulling him out. Mr Bisset also was present, and "spotting" me among the bystanders, instructed his two keepers to order me off, see me out into the main-road, and not leave me until we reached the cross-way, above Hele Bridge. Thus one of my plans was defeated. Instead of ingratiating myself with the master, I had got myself, if that

were possible, still further into his black
books. To me this result was incomprehen-
sible. I did not need to stay there in order
to learn knife-work of Arthur, as I was used
to that myself, and, besides, it was an adver-
tised meet. Even if he objected to me, what
right had Mr Bisset to send me packing?
However, I left very quietly, for, whether
their employer was right or wrong, the keepers,
I knew, were only doing their duty. "But,"
thought I to myself, "Jack shall be as good
as his master," and within a short time of his
disgrace he was. It may have been a week
after this occurrence that I said to my brother:

"Will you have a stroll with me?"

"Yes," he replied; "I don't mind. What
are you up to?"

"Oh, just going round to see if I can knock
down a hare or two," I explained, "or anything
I can get hold of."

So off we started. I was stalking along
under the wood-hedge at Execleave, when
I fancied I heard something on the other side.
Keeping very quiet, I looked in over and saw
a deer eating the ivy off a tree not five yards
from me. I motioned to my brother to remain
still, and myself stepped back into the ditch-

trough. My gun, as it happened, was loaded with shot, but I always carried balls with me. So, holding the gun sideways, to avoid making a noise, I truckled a ball in, and slipped in a bit of paper with the ram-rod—an old stick. Then, with the utmost caution, I crept up the hedge again. It is necessary to be very careful in mounting a hedge, rising slowly, and sometimes inserting your knee. I fired. The shot told, for in a few moments the deer was crawling and struggling down the wood. He had gone about half-way down the side of the hill when we caught him and cut his throat. A brilliant thought now occurred to me. Contrary to my usual procedure, I again took the knife in my hand, and hacked off the stag's head.

"What are you doing that for?" asked my brother.

"I mean to carry it home," was my reply "Better to have some than lose all."

Whereupon I hoisted the trophy on the barrel of my gun and carried it home in broad daylight. Thus and thus I was "up chalks" with Mr Bisset.

One more deer story. A farmer out Hynam way sent a message to Duck Paddle, asking me to come up. A deer, he said, was eating his barley before it was ripe. Accordingly, with another man, I repaired to the farm, and was shown the field. The deer was there, but not within shot. I marked the "rack" or gap by which he had come in over, and said to my companion:

"Go round and drive him back towards me."

Meanwhile, I remained in the wood, whither the stag was sure to betake himself. The device worked well. The deer was frightened, and ran in my direction. On approaching me he appeared to smell something, and paused. There was no time to lose—I fired. He fell, and broke one of his horns. However, after that, he jumped the fence, and proceeded some way into the wood. My companion followed, found the deer lying down, and cut his throat with a hook. We hid him away till night, fetched him home, and the next day sold him out, chiefly to poor people and shopkeepers. As he was a heavy deer—about ten score—we made a good price. I have related this story to show how reasonable some farmers are. The deer was hardly dead, when the old fellow that sent for me remarked:

"You needn't have made such a mess with the barley."

"We made no more than we were obliged to," I retorted. "The deer did it, tumbling about."

Afterwards he found a new grievance.

"You never brought me up a piece of it," he grumbled.

Not likely! I thought myself very kind to do the killing for him, without keeping him supplied with venison. It was a great favour to kill a deer that was eating barley.

CHAPTER VI

HOW I WENT OUT WITH A VIOLENT CHARACTER

FROM what I have read I infer that the general idea of a poacher is that of a desperate ruffian who will do almost anything — kill people, if he is driven into a corner. Nobody who has read these pages will consider me a man of that stamp, and I am greatly mistaken if I have not made an agreeable impression on the reader. " Not a bad sort of chap," he will say, " but, of course, he oughtn't to have been a poacher." Oh no! Being a poacher, however, I acted up to a high standard of conduct. Anyhow, it was always my firm resolve not to hurt anybody, and I never did. " But, perhaps," someone may say, " you have been *associated with* ruffians—regular wicked devils, out-and-out criminals." Well, to be quite honest about it, I have. It takes some little time to find out exactly who is who, and accident may bring you acquainted with undesirable companions, whose society, when you know more of them, you quickly proceed to drop. But I need not maunder on in this way. Poaching, at best, is a rough business, full of various risks, and you can never tell what may turn up. For men like me that is its great charm.

But to my tale. There came to Dulverton Fair — it was the winter fair — a man called Abraham Hake. I suppose he had heard something about me. At any rate, he made inquiries, ascertained where I lived, and left word that I should call to see him. I went. It turned out that he wanted to learn whether I could do some poaching with him. He mentioned also that he required another man, whom I soon got, so as to make three of us. The third man was Charley Chilcott. Entering into conversation, we asked Hake what part of the country he intended visiting. He told us, and we agreed to go. He then gave us certain instructions.

"You must get," he said, "at the first start two pounds of powder, two or three boxes of caps, and a bag of shot."

"What are you going to do with all this?" we asked. We were never accustomed to buy in such quantities.

OUT WITH A VIOLENT CHARACTER

"Stop with me long enough," he answered, "and I'll show you."

It was a two days' fair. On the third day Hake's father and mother, who had ginger-bread standings, went on to Carhampton, a village between Dunster and Williton, to which place they belonged. They made the journey in a trap with a tilt over it to keep out the wet. We followed in the same direction, and by the time we reached Carhampton, had accounted for one-and-twenty birds. On arriving, we found they had no bed for us, but out in the back-house was a lot of ferns; and there, putting the best face on a bad job, we had to lie. Naturally, we did not wish to be seen about, so we slept by day. That, however, was no novelty to me, as it was my ordinary practice when engaged in poaching operations.

About ten o'clock we made a start, proceeding first in the direction of Conegar Tower, the property of Squire Luttrell. There were two guns between three of us; and when we had found our birds, two of us shot the pheasants, while the third picked them up. That night we worked as far as Blue Anchor, and when we thought we had bagged enough we went home. We had agreed with a man of Carhampton, called Griffiths, to take the birds at two shillings each. Every morning, therefore, about nine o'clock, he arrived with a pony and trap, received the pheasants, and drove to Bridgewater. Leaving his pony there he trained up to Bristol, sold the birds, and returned to Carhampton, waiting for another lot.

The following night we made trial of Squire Halliday's preserves. The pheasants there were like rooks, a bird on every tree, and sometimes three or four; so we could kill as many as we liked. We took what we deemed a fair load, and back again. The next night to Lady Egremont's bit of land, shot over her coverts, and killed about the same quantity as before. Then to Sir Peregrine Acland's. Matters went on regularly in this way for three weeks, until I became so familiar with the ground that I could find my way even now easily on the blackest night. You may imagine the havoc we played; in fact, I look upon this as the grand expedition of my life.

At last we ran short of powder. The shopkeepers, we knew, would not put it up in the dark; so I, as the youngest, was chosen to fetch it. I entered a shop, bought a pound of powder, and carried it home. With this fresh supply of ammunition we devastated Sir Peregrine Acland's preserves, meeting with no incident of any kind. However, we had not been in bed very long when we heard "rap, rap," at the door, and on answering the knock the women were faced by three keepers and a couple of constables.

"Who have you here?" they inquired.

"Two men in the outhouse," was the reply.

We jumped up.

"And your husband?"

"He is upstairs in bed."

"Tell him to come down."

Down came Hake, and they proceeded to search the house. They seized two guns, powder-horn, shot-bags, and six-and-twenty pheasants, a fine lot of birds, including sixteen cocks. The constables then hand-bolted me and Abe Hake together, and Rag-gatherer Chilcott to one of their own number, conveyed us to Williton, and summoned a magistrates' meeting. We were made to appear one by one. After the constables had given evidence as to finding the birds, the chairman asked me how I had come by them.

"I was going towards Carhampton from Wheddon Cross," I answered, "and picked them up in the road."

"How were they lying?" was the next question.

"Oh, littered about," I replied, "as if they'd dropped out of a waggon or back of a cart."

"Very strange!" he remarked.

However, they could make nothing of me, and by-and-by they said that would do, and dismissed the case. Upon that we demanded the game and the guns, but they declined to give them up. Thereupon I sent word to my father. He came, and insisted on the property being restored. Otherwise, he said, he should employ legal assistance. This threat sufficed. The police gave way, and everything was handed back to us. After this experience I thought the place too hot to remain any longer, and Chilcott and myself returned to Dulverton with my father. Hake was anxious for us to stop. He told us the affair would blow over in a day or two, and reminded us of our great success — three hundred and eighty-five pheasants in the three weeks. We refused to hearken, and he engaged a fresh mate, someone belonging to the place.

The sequel showed how wise was our resolution. The keepers heard that Hake was about that night, and saw him, and followed him. When he jumped over the gate into the road, one of them was close behind. Hake's blood was up.

"If you come over the stile to me," he said, "I'll blow your brains out."

Undeterred, the keeper advanced. Hake put his gun to his shoulder, and seeing this, the other threw up his arm and ducked his head. My late comrade evidently meant business, for, though he did not blow out the keeper's brains, he shot off his arm. The injured man was Lady Egremont's head-keeper, one Thorn.

Hake now disappeared. For days nothing was heard of him, and he must have been almost starved. At last he was found by two women in an old tallet. One of them gave information, whereupon the police came and arrested him. He was tried, convicted, and sentenced to fifteen years' transportation. On being told of his fate, I said to myself, "A narrow escape for his lordship!"

I referred just now to the various risks, the

"excursions and alarums" of which a poacher's life is full. After the many accounts that I have given, nobody will question either the number or extent of the dangers. It requires a high heart and stout courage to traverse the woods by night at the imminent risk of being pounced on and sent to that detestable place, the common jail. Whatever romance there may be in a man's constitution, you may take it as certain that very few—and this applies more particularly to those who have experienced it—regard with anything but aversion the prospect of being immured for months within the stern precincts of a prison. Good-bye, liberty! good-bye, merry companions! Good-bye, ale and song! However, I do not propose to regale you with any more "catchings," but rather to bring forward some unusual instances of exciting adventure, one or two of which might well have ended in fresh interviews with my friend the turnkey.

My brother, myself, and another man, were shooting pheasants on Sir Thomas Acland's land. The exact locality was Hollam plantation, Winsford. As we made our way through the wood, we came to a tree on which were two pheasants. Wishing to kill them at one shot, we went round, got them in a line, shot and killed both. One fell, the other was suspended in the branches. We searched about for sticks, and tried to knock it down, but did not succeed. My brother now proposed to climb up, which he did, but, in reaching out a long way in order to shake the bird down, broke the limb of the tree, and fell with a crash to the ground. There he lay, as if dead. We picked him up, sought to stand him on his legs, but the attempt was vain.

We were in a terrible fix. It would have been cruel—indeed, it was impossible to leave my brother, and yet to remain indefinitely was perhaps, and more than perhaps, to be caught. We endeavoured to make him understand, and at length he came to himself. We again raised him, but how we got him over the hedge, whether by dragging or lifting him, I positively cannot remember. All I know is that, on our way home he walked between us, we supporting, almost carrying him, and that it was hours before we reached Dulverton. However, we persevered, and finally got to Duck Paddle, where we put the poor chap to bed. It was not Bill the tailor that met with this accident, but a younger brother, a painter and glazier, employed by Mr Davey. The next day his master sent to inquire why he had not come to work as usual.

"Oh, please say," said father and mother in a breath, "he has fallen downstairs and hurt his back, so he can't come."

This explanation had, of course, been pre-arranged at a family council. In point of fact, not one day, nor two days, but several weeks elapsed before he was strong enough to resume his occupation, and he ought to have been thankful that he resumed it at all.

On Mr Lucas's estate were two little places —Daw's and Delbridge's—both of which were used as dairies. Pheasants were fairly plentiful round there, and I knew where they went to feed—namely, to some ricks of corn. I paid a visit to the spot, and looking through the hedge, saw that I could have but one bird at a shot. I shot, killed one, and, as my custom was, immediately took abroad my gun. I then advanced, picked up the pheasant, and was putting it in my pocket, when, glancing back over the field, I saw a man riding towards me as hard as ever he could tear. It was Tom Webber of Shircombe. Now Tom was a great hunter, especially of stags. Tall (nearly six foot high), with black, curly hair, he was a large farmer, renting under Mr Lucas, and was probably looking after his stock, when, as luck would have it, he caught sight of me.

I went "for my blood and eyes." He followed, and I could not possibly have escaped if only he had brought his horse to jumping. As it was, when he arrived at the gate, he found it bound, and this gave me another start. I reached the bottom of the next field, looked round. He was coming. Fortunately down there was a wood, and, when I had descended on the other side of the hedge, I felt myself safe. "Good-bye, old fellow!" I cried, crossed the river, and away to the friendly shades of Stockham plantation. Mr Webber could not have recognised me, or I should have been prosecuted.

Singularly enough the same afternoon, as I was trying Stockham ground, I noticed two men clearly in pursuit of me. I deemed discretion the better part of valour, or, as we express the idea in west country phrase, thought it better for the legs to run than the body to perish. There was no peace anywhere, so I went home without attempting to hold conversation with them, which might have cost me thirty shillings or a couple of pounds. I mention this coincidence as a sort of fatality, for I cannot recollect being "coursed" twice on the same day either before or since.

I will next relate a much stranger incident that befell me when out poaching. I was stalking the wood at Shircombe Slade, intending to kill a hare—hares were very abundant in that direction — when I saw something behind the bushes, and could not imagine what it was. It appeared to me pretty much like the devil. When it saw me, it kept throwing up its hand, and, as it were, beckoning to me. I did not know what to do about going up to him. At last, however, I made an offer at it. I had my gun in my hand, ready-loaded, and I thought, even if it were the devil, he stood the worse chance of the two. It continued throwing up its hand, and I drew nearer and nearer, until I came within hearing distance. Then the object spoke.

"What!" said he, "don't you know me? My name's Jack Cordwain."

"How was it possible for me to know you," I answered, "dressed in that disguise, and a smutty face, too. What makes you rig yourself out in that fashion?"

OUT WITH A VIOLENT CHARACTER

"So that nobody may know me," he replied.

He had on an old greatcoat, reaching nearly down to his feet, of the pattern people use in driving. I can assure you I was very glad to make friends with him, as I had been in great fear I should be walked off—I mean, carried away. We killed two or three hares, after which he went down to the river, washed his face, packed up his greatcoat, and tied it up in a handkerchief. When he had performed his toilet, we went home together.

Cordwain was a terrible fellow to run, and could jump over any gate without touching it. His strength and fleetness enabled him to accomplish a feat which, in the Exmoor country, is still referred to with admiration. At Winsford Fair there used to be a pleasant custom of putting up a sheep to run for. The sheep was bedecked with a bunch of ribbons tied round its neck, and its tail shaved and greased. The competitors had to seize the animal, not by the leg, but by its greasy tail, which was, of course, not particularly easy to retain. The sheep was let go, about a mile from the village, on a common called Bye, which was full of dreadful bottoms. The animal knew its bounds, and sometimes went miles before it was eventually caught. It is remembered of Cordwain that, under these hard conditions, he caught the sheep in full course.

This brings me to the subject of my own recreations, and the way I disposed of my money. I was very fond of going about to fairs and revels, where wrestling and similar amusements were in vogue. At Bridgtown, a village between Dulverton and Minehead, there was an annual revel, at which prizes were offered for grinning through a horse's collar, jumping in bags, and the like, and wrestling and fighting were all the go. Not that I was a champion wrestler or fighter. Sometimes, however, I got into it, and came away with black eyes, or sore legs, and naturally the worse for drink. In those days horse-races were held at various places in the neighbourhood—on Northmoor first, and afterwards at Brushford, in the space now occupied by the Carnarvon Arms. There was no hotel then, and no railway station, but there was always a drinking booth.

Well, of course, I must go to the races, and, once at the races, it was equally necessary that I should "booze." Whilst "boozing" I got into some bother with a Dulverton man, and we began wrestling and iteming. I fell, or he threw me, and I dislocated my neck. Blood streamed from my ears, and a man, putting his knee to my shoulder, pulled my neck into its proper place. That, at all events, was what was told me. I cannot speak from personal knowledge, as I was insensible at the time. They were forced to carry me home, but without calling in a doctor, I managed to get right.

Soon after I had put out my neck at the races, there happened to be a venison feast at the Red Lion. This is an annual dinner given to the farmers of the district, in consideration of their preserving deer, and it has been instituted, I believe, for quite a century. The feast takes place in October, and they kill their deer for the occasion. I have understood that the farmers do uncommonly well at these feasts, being generally good trencher-men. In this respect, I daresay I should not have been far behind ; but, as I was a deer-destroyer rather than a deer-preserver, I was never invited, and so my powers were not put to the test. Well, I suppose they had finished dinner, and gone through the usual routine of

toasting and being toasted, when up jumped
an old farmer and said:

"I hear that deer-killer Holcombe has put
out his neck. I wish he had broken it, and
made a good job of the business."

"What, what?" replied Mr Bisset, "don't you
know that he is flesh and blood as much as
ourselves?"

I conclude, therefore, that the water ran down
Mr Bisset's back rather cold; he didn't care
for such ferocity. The subject was speedily
hushed up, and, whereas the old man had expected three cheers, he got no response.
Everybody was intent on something else. I
can imagine, too, that the farmer thought that
Mr Bisset would have sent Arthur Heal with
an extra piece of venison, or Maynard with
a brace of pheasants, but, as regards that, I
am bound to confess that the old man was
perfectly capable of killing his own pheasants.
However, in spite of his kind wishes, I have
lived long enough to see him put to bed with
a shovel, as well as poor Mr Bisset. Mr Bisset
and I were very often at loggerheads, but,
nevertheless, he was a man I respected. He
was the finest man that ever hunted the stag,
or ever will, and in that way was a supporter

of the district. Were it not for the stag-hunting and the fishing, Dulverton would be as poor as Bampton. I went down through there one morning, and I saw one poor solitary man keeping up the "derns" of a door with his shoulders. He looked to me as if a dinner would have done him good.*

A year passed, and there were races again. I felt I must go, following up my old tricks. So down I went, drank like the rest, and nothing particular occurred until night. I then got into another scrape, fighting with some man whom I don't know, and broke my leg. This was a bad job, worse than the dislocation, and some Dulverton men, having procured a hurdle, brought me to Duck Paddle. Mr John Collyns, son of the old doctor, was sent for to set my leg, and soon arrived. He seasoned the operation with good advice.

"I should think, John," he said, "you would leave off poaching now."

"Not I," I replied, "if I get right again."

"I suppose," he went on, "you get a lot of

---

* Local prejudice. Since the revival of the quarries Bampton has been doing well. It is even attracting some of the tourist element.—CARACTACUS.

money from poaching, and that is how you go about to these sort of places."

"Yes," I said, "and, as long as there's any game going, I mean to have it."

I don't know whether it was owing to my poaching propensities, but it seemed to me that the doctor served my leg very bad in setting it—pulling and hauling away till I could have fairly screeched. When he had finished, he turned and said:

"My advice to you, John, is to do no more to it."

Speaking of the Brushford races, a much more serious accident once happened in connection with them—I believe, on the first occasion of their being held. Over our drinking-place— Blake's—was a stand. Not the grand stand, which was in another part of the field, opposite to it, but, nevertheless, it was crowded with spectators. This stand appears to have been constructed of old rotten timber from Riphay, where a new house had just been built, and it collapsed. Higgledy-piggledy, down it came, the people all in a heap. Amongst the victims was a Mrs Pulsford, who was carried away on a hurdle. The crowd rushed to the spot, and Mr Locke of Northmoor stood whip in hand, ordering them to keep back, so as to enable the luckless ones to extricate themselves and others to aid them. With the exception of Mrs Pulsford, however, I do not remember that there were any bad cases.

The races lasted two days, and, besides the usual events, there were miscellaneous items, such as running for a slop, donkey-racing for a bridle, etc. Women, also, ran for gown-pieces, and the Gages of King's Brompton—young ladies not yet forgotten in the neighbour-hood—always won.

In addition to these performances—athletic sports they would be called now, I suppose—there were such diversions as smoking for a cheese. Half-an-ounce of tobacco was assigned to each competitor, and he was watched by a man who saw that the pipe was properly burnt out, and nothing left but ashes. Once, at Winsford Fair, I won a waistcoat by smoking. I say a waistcoat, for that was the way it was put. In reality it was a square piece of cloth not worth making up, and decidedly not worth the trouble, seeing that my mouth was like a furnace, and ready to catch fire with the exercise.

Mention of waistcoats reminds me of what

befell a new jacket I had made for the express purpose of poaching in it. It was of fustian, and all down through on both sides were pockets, deep enough to prevent the contents from falling out — one for the barrel of the gun, the other for the stock. The purchase was made about Anstey revel time, and as I was not at all indifferent to appearances, I thought I must put on my new coat in order to be seen in it.

As revels are now things of the past, it may interest you to learn what they were like. They were institutions maintained by the innkeepers or some jolly old squire, and the programme was chiefly wrestling, drinking, and, later in the day, dancing. Plenty of fun went on, not always very proper, but people were not so particular then, except perhaps a few Methodists, who had high jinks of another description. As regards prizes, sometimes money was offered, not a large sum, sometimes only an old hat with the fur an inch long. This hat was provided by the landlord of the public-house, and on the Sunday preceding the revel was worn to Church, with a bunch of ribbons streaming from it, by the head or champion wrestler. Three backs in succession qualified for a prize, and I am ashamed to say that this was often a matter of cheating and collusion. Those of the same place—Dulverton, for instance—would agree beforehand to "play," if possible, with each other. The winner would be decided on, and, after show of kicking and grabbling, the others would allow themselves to be thrown. Then the money, what little there was, would be divided between us. In order that the game might succeed, it was necessary to be quick, and toss your hat into the ring, before a man belonging to some other place had time to challenge the winner.

I forget whether I had made such a compact on the occasion in question. At all events, when I got to the field, I found wrestling had begun, and threw in my hat to play against somebody. I took off my new jacket and laid it down outside, feeling sure that it would be taken care of. When, however, I came out of the wrestling, I discovered that some dishonest person had taken a fancy to it. It was nowhere to be seen, and I never had it afterwards.

Well, now I think I have shown pretty clearly how the stag-money and the game-money used to go, but there is still one matter on which I can throw light. I was reminded of it by what

AUTOBIOGRAPHY OF A POACHER

I said in the last story about men of the same place holding together. They not only held together, but kept up feuds with other towns and villages ; and every town and village in our part of the world thought itself the best.

A Brompton man recalled to me not long ago a foolish old rhyme that circulated in some by-places, not in Dulverton—

> " Hawkridge cocks, Withypool hens,
> Dulverton boys, Brompton men."

As if, forsooth, we were no better than boys compared with the great lusty fellows bred up at King's Brompton ! We were encompassed with enemies. Sometimes the Winsford men got fighting with us. We reckoned ourselves superior, but, before we had finished, some of us were well polished. When the Bury men came into town and those of Dulverton kicked up a row, the villagers used to "dray their adder-killers"—*i.e.* their knives. This was done, no doubt, to redress the advantage caused by our numbers. We of Dulverton did not wait to count heads, but chased intruders, whether few or many. Naturally, however, as ours was a bigger place, we were always, or nearly always, in a majority. The only exception was Bampton, then a thriving town of about the same size, and containing a decent lot of chaps that knew how to handle their fists. The Dulverton men used to go down to Exe Bridge, about midway between the rival towns and right on the borders of Devon and Somerset, and there fight pitched battles with the Turnip Greens. We called the Bampton foe by that name, because of a tradition that they were permitted to go into a field and pick turnip-greens in a bed-tick, and couldn't get out at the gate.

London people would no doubt call us Dulverton fellows rustics, but we always drew a line between those living in the town and farm-hands. These bumpkins we of Dulverton despised heartily, and I can recall at least one occasion when an overweening conceit of myself and contempt for others cost me pretty dear.

A country chap, who lived at a place called Chilcott, about two miles from here, had a maid—I mean, a sweetheart—in Dulverton, where she was in service. I saw him walking this girl, and resolved to take her away. This was a common dodge at Dulverton, one of our favourite larks, to deprive country fellows of their maids. We did it, not by persuasion, which might have been fair play, but—it was too bad—by force. Well, as they were crossing Barle Bridge, I overtook them and carried off the girl, much to Georgie Lock's disgust, though, I am bound to say, the young woman herself was not unwilling to come with me. After some words George went home, and I was left cock of the walk.

However, during the week he sent me a message, proposing that we should fight it out and so decide which should have her. The challenge did not alarm me in the least, as I was confident that it would not take me long to beat a country fellow. Accordingly, I replied that I was ready to fight him, and desired to know where we were to meet. He sent word that he would come half-way —to Old Shute—if that would suit me. I answered "Yes," and the time of the encounter was fixed—viz. a certain night.

Now if I had given the matter only a few minutes' consideration, I should not have regarded the prospect with indifference, and even pleasure, for Lock, though short, was stiff-grown and quite capable, with a fair field and no favour, of acquitting himself well. I have seen in the paper lately that a foreign

OUT WITH A VIOLENT CHARACTER

gentleman—a statesman, I suppose—considers
that prestige is forty per cent. of power. That
was my idea, but things did not turn out exactly
as I anticipated. In fact, though I did not know
it, I was in for the biggest fight of my life.

About twenty accompanied me from Dulverton, and Lock brought with him two or three
backers. On our arrival there, he was all in
readiness. He had a man to pick him up,
and I had a man to pick me up; and it was
understood on both sides that there was to
be fair play, and nobody to interfere. We
stripped (shirt and all), shook hands, and
got at it. I still thought I should beat him
in ten minutes, but I soon found I had a
rough bone to tackle. We fought away, and
no doubt, from a spectator's point of view,
it was capital sport. When one or other
was down, we had a rest, sitting on our
backers' knees who "muched us down," push-
ing back our hair, which was worn long in
those days, wiping off the blood, and
generally, wheedling us on. Several times I
got him by the head, and hit him up, but
he was perfectly game, and the fight went
on for over an hour. (One hour and five
minutes, I think they said.)

AUTOBIOGRAPHY OF A POACHER

At last we were both fagged out, and the backers, seeing that neither of us was any good, suggested that we should stop and fight again the following week. To this we agreed, but, when the next week came, there was no sign of a fight, as we were both thoroughly afraid of each other. And no wonder. He had knocked my thumb out of joint, and I was in such a state that I had to stay in bed for several days, while he, black and blue all over, could not go to work. I fancy you will ask me, what about the maid? To be candid, I thought no more about her; and whether she went with Lock or kept to herself I neither knew nor cared. What I did, I did for roguery, and on reflection I must admit that I was well paid for my pains.

It was not all harmony even at Dulverton. Fairs, and revels, and pitched battles were, of course, only occasional; and at ordinary times, if we wanted to amuse ourselves, it was often by playing pitch-halfpenny outside the chapel, or, on Sundays, in some by-linhay. Then there was always that great resource — the public-house. No law then compelled the landlord to close at the early hour of ten, and if he thought it worth while he would keep in a fire for our convenience, while we stayed up all night playing cards. There would generally be two or three encounters owing to accusations of cheating—some fellow would have a card up his sleeve — and then the landlord would threaten to turn us out. Not unfrequently the party broke up in a bother of this sort. One of our favourite meeting-places was kept by an old dame, who was very stingy. If we had herrings for supper, and threw the heads under the table, she would pick them up and eat them. Not much of a scholar, she used to chalk up debts on the mantelpiece — one stroke for a pint. We played all sorts of games with her—some of them too bad for mention. One of the most innocent was to hide away something left on the table, when she went out to draw beer. So, too, if there were meat in the crock, we would fish it out. By-and-by she would go to the crock, find nothing there, and nobody would know anything about it. Capital!

Christmas - tide, however, in most places is the principal season for enjoyment, and in our part of the world many of the labouring people got hardly any other holiday, except on Good

Friday. Old Christmas Day is generally observed, and plenty of men religiously decline to take out their teams when it comes round. To do the farmers justice, they have never stinted hospitality at Christmas-tide, but, as I was not a farmer's man, I only came in for that kind of pleasure *accidentally*. It was like this. A certain number of young Dulverton chaps used to act a play. "Mummers" is the proper name for such performers, but they were known as "Christmas boys," and the chief character was old Father Christmas. He used to be got up as a venerable old fellow, with a long white beard and a big cloak. He had a bad cough, and had to support his tottering footsteps with a staff. He and his party were always welcome visitors at farmhouses, and whilst the inmates sat round a comfortable fire, we actors were introduced one by one and went through our parts. First Old Father Christmas entered, saying,

" Here come I, Old Father Christmas.
    Welcome here, or welcome not,
    Old Father Christmas never shall be forgot.

" A room, a room for sport,
    In this house I mean to resort,
    Pastime and merry play,
    Walk in, Mother Christmas, and boldly clear the way."

OUT WITH A VIOLENT CHARACTER

Then I appeared, with the words,

> " Here come I, Old Dame Dorothy,
> Fair, fat, and gomarothy.
> My head is big, and my body is small ;
> I'm the biggest little wench among you all."

Whereupon we would go whopping each other, I using my broom and he his staff, till I was forced to fall down dead, and the chorus sang,

> " Oh see, oh see what thou hast done.—
> Cut down our mother like the evening sun."

A physician was summoned and came, saying,

> " I'm the Spanish doctor,
> I cure the palsy and the gout,
> Pains within and pains without.
> If the devil's in 'em, I'll fetch him out."

Approaching Dame Dorothy, he put a bottle to the old woman's nose, remarking,

> " Here, Dame, take a drop of my flip-flop
> In thy tip-top.
> Rise, Joan, and tell one what time 'tis."

Then, reviving, I answered,

" Half-past thirteen ; when it comes to fourteen it'll strike."

The next personage was a foreign potentate.

" Here come I, the King of Egypt, plainly doth appear ;
St George is my only son and heir.
Walk in, St George, and boldly act thy part,
And all the glorious company shall see thy noble art."

153

Accordingly, St George entered, saying,

> "Here come I, St George, St George,
> That did from England spring,
> With all my mighty works and fortunes to begin."

He reckoned up all that he had performed, concluding with the statement that he had slain the dragon and rescued the King of Egypt's daughter. He was immediately challenged by a foe:

> "Here come I, the Turkish Knight,
> Come from the Turkish lands to fight.
> Fight him I will, if I am slain."

They set to, saying to each other,

> "Give a point, take a point."

Then, I think, came the Devil.

> "Here come I, Old Belzebub,
> On my shoulder I carry my club,
> In my hand a dripping pan,
> Don't you think I'm a jolly old man?"

Other characters were St Valentine, Orsin and his bear, and there was also the Trial and Execution of Admiral Byng, in which a number of sailors were introduced, and an old fowling-piece was fired, sometimes with rock powder, which caused a disagreeable smell. I fear I cannot remember more of the dialogue, as, of course, I had only to learn my own part, but the specimens I have quoted will give you an idea of what our Christmas Play was like forty or fifty years ago.

Did you ever hear of women poaching? Probably not. Well, I have. I cannot say that I have ever met any of the sex engaged in this way, but I have it on good authority that instances of the sort are not unknown, though doubtless rare. On one occasion my father and brother were night - hunting in Dulverton parish, and decided to try a certain field. When they came to the gate, they found a woman standing there with a net tilled. She was a farmer's daughter, young, tall, and strapping, with light hair and fresh complexion. Altogether, a very attractive specimen.

"What are you doing here?" asked my father.

"The same kind of work you are going about," she replied. "My brother is down in the bottom."

Saying this she took up her net, and went down across the field. My father, who knew the family, followed and entered into conversation with the brother. They agreed to go, one in one direction, and the other in another,

155

so as not to disturb each other. When father came back, he said to me:

"Jack, if you had been with us you would have seen a woman night-hunting."

"Ah!" I replied, "I should have liked that."

And so I should, but I was "boozing" that night, and, so long as I had money, you would not catch me night-hunting.

At another time, when I did not happen to be with them, they were night-hunting in Anstey parish, and came across a man and woman indulging in the same pursuit. They met the woman first, and, woman-like, she ran away. My brother bolted after her, and caught her. On overtaking the couple, he recognised them as acquaintances. Thereupon they wished each other good-night, and both parties went their own way.

There is an old saying:

"A woman, a dog, and a walnut tree,
  The more you beat 'em, the better they be."

I hope it will not be thought very impolite, therefore, if I go from women to dogs. The anecdote is worth relating, as it will show what hares were like in those days. Well, one Sunday about twelve o'clock, my father and I set off with the dog and nets. We first

OUT WITH A VIOLENT CHARACTER

visited Perry, a farm on Lord Carnarvon's estate, tried two or three fields, and then went on to Pixton hill. We caught nine hares and a rabbit, with nets, and by four o'clock we were at home. In returning the dog took after one of the park deer. Whether he knocked over the deer, or the deer kicked him, I am unable to say. Anyhow, he came back with a broken leg, and, to get him home, we had to carry him. The next day we bandaged the leg, procured an elder-stick, split it into two parts, hollowed out the middles, put the splints on each side of the dog's leg, got a good long wax thread, tied the splints with it, and after a time the dog became all right again. However, he was spoilt for that season, a circumstance we much regretted, as he was a lurcher, or biggish terrier, trained to sport, and used for driving deer.

When I first went night-hunting with my father, we had a little bitch whose name was Fury, a smooth-haired, black-and-tan terrier, standing about fifteen inches. Coming to a field that we proposed to try, we would raise the corner of the net to let her in. The bitch would go inside the gate, and if no hare was there, would drop her nose. We have proved that bitch. Thinking that there were hares about, we have entered, run all over the field, lit paper, just to see if she was false, but never found any mistake. She always told right. Going on to the next field, she would perhaps cock her nose, and then there would be no holding her. There was a hare in the field. I have watched that bitch and seen her go straight as a line to a hare, when she would "quest" (*i.e.* bark very small) about twice.

A dog must not break a hedge, and if properly trained, will seek to work a hare so as to drive her to the gate. If a dog broke a hedge, it was customary to put on him what was called a "check" collar, with little spikes inside. To this collar was attached about fifteen yards of good stiff line, at the other end of which was a stick, say two feet long. When he went over the hedge, the stick would catch in the bushes, the dog would have to stop, and then I gave him a hiding. This was a capital plan, of my own invention, and when I was a keeper I have broken a good many pointers and setters that way.

Our little Fury needed no "check" collar, as she was perfection. Many a long night we have been out with that bitch, coursing hares, and I have known her so tired that my father has carried her home in his arms, ten or twelve miles. After we had worked her for ten years, she began to get stiff, and we thought we must have a fresh dog. Accordingly, she was put to a greyhound, and had a litter of pups. We picked out the dog we fancied, and named him Tear 'em. As he grew up, we took him out with the old bitch to bring him to the same cleverness in poaching. When the dog, seeing his mother's manœuvres, came to know the ropes, we killed the bitch, then quite worn out. As we were so fond of her, the necessity caused us deep pain, and not wishing to witness her dying struggles, we hung her up and left her. The new dog turned out a proper beauty. He could go even faster than the old one, but he could not catch a hare in full course. However, he could keep up with a hare, and prevent her from breaking a hedge. We worked Tear 'em for years, and he was a splendid dog. We had a lot of other dogs, but none like those two. When I left home, father got rid of him, and there was an end of that.

CHAPTER VII

I CHANGE MY CALLING

I HAVE now pretty well completed my account of my poaching career, and it will, I think, be generally regarded as a memorable one. Now and then I am reminded of incidents that I had almost totally forgotten. For instance, the clerk that wrote out this book tells me that a Withypool farmer remembers a scene in court after one of my convictions. It appears that I was obstreperous, and Constable Fisher and myself rolled on the floor, he attempting to handcuff me, and I resisting. On another occasion, my sister informs me, my conduct was so desperate that I had to be tied down with ropes in a cart, and thus conveyed to Taunton. I have no recollection of the journey, which must have been very unpleasant, but I have an indistinct remembrance of an order being given to this effect by the magistrates. So, I suppose, that may be taken as corroborative evidence.

I CHANGE MY CALLING

Coming to my transition from a poacher to a gamekeeper, the accepted account in Dulverton is that the magistrates, discouraged by my frequent appearances before them (which, however, they knew bore but a small proportion to my poaching forays), laid their heads together and decided to resort to any means in order to rid the country of me. On fully considering the matter — so it is said — they determined to make a gamekeeper of me, or, at any rate, to offer me the chance of becoming one. If this story is correct—I, for my part, doubt it — the magistrates certainly showed good sense. A learned gentleman—the same I mentioned before—has given me some lines from an old English poet called Chaucer, and they are very much to the point:

"A thief of venison that hath for-left
His licorousness, and all his thief's craft,
Can keep a forest best of any man."

No doubt of it, and my belief is that it was admiration of my talents, more than a desire to banish me from Dulverton, that led my late honoured master to engage my services. I am the more persuaded of this from the fact that for some time—probably a year—I had been living a quiet life, pit - sawing in different

L   161

woods; and though we had wires and picked
up a pheasant or two going to work morning-
times, what did that amount to? It was a
flea-bite, compared with my former exploits.
Perhaps, however, I may as well mention
my last performance in this line. We were
sawing at Mouncey Farm when we saw two
or three pheasants flying round a rick. It
happened that we had no caps with us, so
we sent Tom Berry to Mr Smith with the
request that he would lend us caps, as we
wanted to shoot some wild ducks. Mr
Smith was complaisant, lent us the caps, and,
going round the rick, we killed one of the
pheasants.

Then there was a turn of the scale. At a
magistrates' meeting a man—old Tom Quick—
came to me and said:

"You must please go up to the Red Lion, a
gentleman wishes to see you. Don't be longer
than five minutes, as he is in a hurry."

Tom Quick used to accompany gentlemen,
when they went fishing, carrying their bags,
etc. I had therefore no doubt that the message
was genuine, but still I could not divine what
business the sender could possibly have with
me. I went home to tidy up, and I suppose

had an air of mystery about me, for my poor old mother exclaimed :

"What have you been up to? Been caught again and haven't told of it ? " I was the "treaty-bird" of the family, and she was afraid of her life I should go for a soldier. As soon as I was decent, I repaired to the Red Lion, was called inside, and, lo and behold! there stood Mr Barnett of Morebath House.

"Good-morning, Holcombe!" he said. "Would you like to be a gamekeeper?"

The question took me all of a hop, and for a minute or two it was as much as ever I could speak. However, I replied,

"Yes, sir, very well, but on what terms?"

He gave me an idea of the terms, and then said,

"You are not married?"

"No," I answered.

"Well," he observed, "if you'll go, come to my house on such and such a day." I went, and settled matters with him. I found I was not to be employed at Morebath, a place within easy reach of Dulverton, but on an estate near Honiton, in Devon. We arranged what day I should start, and Mr Barnett said he would send down his steward to get lodgings for me at

163

Combe Raleigh. He gave me money to pay my fare, and instructed me where to go for a gun, as well as powder and shot. These points having been determined, I took leave, well pleased with the gentleman and myself.

At the appointed time, I set out. My brother and I walked all the way, starting very early and arriving about six o'clock. I called at the steward's, and he conducted me to my lodging, promising to show me some of the outbounds the next day. On the morrow I rose in good time, and, according to arrangement, went over part of the estate with the steward. On the third day I had a stroll by myself. Going to a certain plantation, I looked across, and saw two men ferreting. I slipped down towards them. They saw me, and away they went, leaving ferret, nets, and a big bed of earth. I continued to follow, noticing which, they parted, and made off in opposite directions. I was now forced to confine my attention to one. After running half-a-mile I overtook him, and found he had but one arm.

"What is your name?" I asked.

"John Webber," he replied.

"Where do you live?" I asked again.

"At Awliscombe," he answered.

I CHANGE MY CALLING

"Come," said I. "I am a stranger in these parts, and that isn't good enough for me. I shall go to Awliscombe with you."

On we went, and by-and-by I saw a man in a field, ploughing. I hailed him.

"Will you please tell me who this man is?" I inquired.

"John Webber, sir," was the reply.

"H'm!" I thought, "that sounds plausible," but even so I was not satisfied. I could see, or, at any rate, I guessed, that the fellow was well-known in the neighbourhood as a thorough old poacher, and everybody seemed to be laughing. However, we did not stop till we came to the village. There was a public-house in the place, and by this time, I can assure you, I was wanting a drink. We entered, and I said to the landlord,

"What is the name of this man?"

"John Webber," he answered.

On receiving this reply, I concluded that, if all called him John Webber, John Webber he must be. Accordingly, when I had had a pint of beer, I gave him his freedom, and went back a mile or two to the spot where I first saw them, and I had left the nets. I picked up the nets, but could see no signs of the ferret. I knew what to do. Close by was a farmhouse belonging to Mr Barnett, and, going to the farmer, I explained to him the situation. We agreed to take some straw, push it into the holes, and fire it, the intention being to smoke the ferret which had " lain." The plan succeeded, for after a time it came out. I now inquired of the farmer if he would keep the ferret until the case was decided.

" Yes," he said, " I'll keep it."

I sent word to Mr Barnett, and by his instructions the man was summoned. When he appeared before the magistrates, the chairman observed,

" What, you again, John ? "

I cannot tell you how oddly the words sounded. They put me in mind of my former self, the place whence I had come, of all that I had done. Webber was found guilty, and as he had no means of paying the fine, was sent to prison for a month. As this was mainly my doing, it was turning the tables with a vengeance.

With regard to the other man, I could never glean any information about him.

After that I rubbed along like any other gamekeeper. I found game very scarce, particularly hares, but there were thousands of

rabbits. Just as I had been a proper poacher,
so now I resolved to be a proper gamekeeper,
and levy war upon night-hunters. I communicated with my master, and inquired whether it
was his pleasure that I should "rap up" all the
gates, so as to prevent the hares from coming
out. He replied : "By all means." In obedience
to orders, I hired a carpenter, caused a lot of
wood to be sawn, and went to work. It took
weeks and weeks to fortify all the gates on the
estate, but at last our task was completed. I
took this course, not knowing whether there were
night-hunters or no, as a measure of precaution.
After a while we found the benefit of it, hares
becoming fairly plentiful. The improvement
affected not only hares, but pheasants. During
our first season, we shot no more than thirty
or forty, but, as time went on, their numbers
increased. Meanwhile I destroyed hundreds of
vermin—crows, magpies, stoats, fitches, etc.—
and got into hot water with the old ladies for
winging their pet cats. One old woman dragged
me by my whiskers through the village. Another
said, "Never mind, he won't eat a peck of salt
here"—meaning that I should not stay long
enough. In this she proved to be mistaken.
I stayed on, year in, year out; game abounded,

and my master, Mr Barnett, was very well pleased. When a stranger arrived on a visit, and they went out shooting, he would mention what I had been, and both would laugh at his stories behind my back. However, you must not think my adventures ended.

One night I was standing on a hill when I heard a shot fired. I went in the direction from which the sound proceeded, and saw a man running away. I gave chase and caught him. The moon was shining clearly, and by its light I found I had got the one-armed man again.

"Well, Jack," I said, "I've caught you once more, then?"

"Caught me in what?" he replied.

"Why, you've just had a shot, haven't you?" I answered; "where's your gun?"

"Haven't got any," he said.

I took him to the nearest cottage, and called up the occupier—a workman. The fellow got out of bed, and, when he came down, I asked him to take charge of Webber for awhile. Lest, however, he should let him escape, I borrowed the man's key, and locked them both in the house. I then went out to look for the gun. As I have said, it was a beautiful moonlight night, and there appeared to be a good prospect of finding the missing weapon. I was not disappointed. In getting over a hedge whence, as I considered, the report came, I espied something glistening. It was the old man's gun, and beside it lay a dead rabbit. I returned to the house, unlocked the door, entered, and searched him. He had a little powder and shot wrapped up in paper, a few caps, and an old pipe, which, it was my opinion, he used in loading.

"It is a bad job, John," I said; "you'll have to go to Honiton with me."

"All right," he replied, "but I hope you'll let me have a drink."

I was quite willing, but the public-houses were closed. However, I called to the land-lord of a house known as the Combe Raleigh Inn, because it was frequented by Combe Raleigh people. Its proper name was the "Red Cow." The landlord, a great big fellow called Robert Parker, came down, and recognised me. He knew us both very well. I asked him to give us something to eat, and something to drink.

"What have you been doing then, John?" inquired Mr Parker, addressing my companion.

"I don't know," he answered. "It depends

on what they have to say about me, I believe."
He finished his supper, and we took him
to the police-station, where he was detained
for the night. The next day he was brought
before the magistrates for night poaching. It
was the old story.

"You've come again, John?"

"Yes."

The case was tried, I was the principal witness,
and they gave him three months. The question
now was, what was I to do with the gun? I
asked the bench, and was told I could do what
I liked with it. I decided to sell it. It was
an old thing, and, to judge from its look, was
not worth five shillings, but, anyhow, that was
the amount I received for it.

The change from poaching to "keepering"
made me an object of dislike to the class with
whom I had hitherto been popular, and once
or twice I had to pay the penalty for my
desertion. One day I went into Honiton and
called at the Three Tuns, a hostelry kept by
Joe Summers, who was also a mason, and did
all the masoning for Combe Raleigh manor.
My reason was this: the landlord was to
put up a leg of mutton to be played for at
skittles. I took part, as I intended, and all

went pleasantly enough whilst we were in the bowling alley. When we had finished bowling we adjourned to the kitchen. I was standing by the mantelpiece before the big chimney-range when all at once I felt something between my legs, and, putting down my hand, drew it right along a red-hot poker. Although distracted with pain, I knew the culprit must have been somebody behind me, and hit out at the first man, right or wrong, knocking him against the settle. From what I was afterwards told, I don't think I was very far wrong. However, the whole party was up in arms, and fell aboard me. They got me down on my back, and played up all sorts of works beyond my power to describe, until the landlord interfered and rescued me. As I did not bargain for a repetition of the incident, I pretended I couldn't walk, and Summers and another man saw me home. Besides bruises, I had a fine pair of black eyes, and my hand remained bad for weeks, so that I could not pull a trigger or make any other use of it. It was very imprudent in me to venture among them, as I had caught one or two of them recently, and might therefore have anticipated some act of revenge.

On another occasion a pigeon-shooting match was to be held at the Royal Oak, a public-house kept by Albion Quick at Lipput, a village about three miles from Honiton. This time the prize was a goose. My landlord and myself attended, and, as luck would have it, I won the prize. I suppose the other competitors did not like my having the goose, and the fact of my being a keeper no doubt told against me. At all events, I saw enough to convince me that I was likely to be in for a good hiding. The publican told me what was brewing; and my own landlord said to me:

"You'll be having it before you go home."

It had got late as we sat drinking, and when drink gets up in the head, then quarrelling begins. Moreover, as I have intimated, the fellows were rather "raw" because I was going to have the goose. So, leaving the goose behind, we slipped away out at the back door, and, getting into a pig's-stye, slept till day-break on some old straw-stuff. Drunken chaps don't care where they sleep. My companion's wife, however, wondered where we were, and was in a dreadful way, poor thing!

Some time after I caught one of those "nabs," who, I thought, would kick up the row, in the

I CHANGE MY CALLING

Red Cow at Honiton, and gave *him* a good hiding. But I was forced to keep away from Lipput for a bit.

Before I got married, I had some peculiar experiences with the young women, and I daresay my readers—particularly the ladies—may like to hear about them. Perhaps they will not approve of my conduct entirely, but, whatever stories I may repeat, there will at least be nothing vulgar in them. The episodes occurred during the time I was keepering. In taking me round to show me the outbounds, coverts, copses, etc., the old steward at Combe Raleigh called at almost every house, and introduced me by saying:

"Here's the new keeper."

Meanwhile, I had got my eyes open for a girl. At last we came to his own brother's cottage, where we entered, and the old man introduced me to two fine young women. In fact, they asked him to usher his friend in.

"I suppose, uncle, you'll have a drop of cider," said one of them; "I don't know whether this young man drinks cider."

"Oh yes," was the reply, "he has drunk along with me this morning."

Thereupon, the tallest of the girls took a

173

jug, went out at the front door, and round the house to a place at the back, where she drew the cider. Then she brought it in, and sat down. I kept blinking at her, and noticed her eyes "purdling," though she pretended not to look. When we had drunk up the cider, she asked:

"Will you have a drop more, uncle?"

"I don't mind," he answered. "I daresay the keeper and me could drink another drop."

So, taking the jug, she stole out to draw some more, and I followed to see where she went to. I found her in a kind of cellar drawing cider, and when she rose up, I said:

"I suppose, miss, you are engaged, aren't you?"

"Not for the present," she said.

"No doubt you have a father and mother," I went on.

"My mother's dead," she answered, "but I have a father. He's a sawyer, and works on the manor, so that he's away every day, and almost all day."

I thought to myself, "That's capital."

"Well," I said, "I daresay I shall look in on my rounds to-morrow."

The next day, about ten o'clock in the

174

morning I called and found her by herself.
Her sister had gone to town; it was no great
distance. This time I had a proper view of
her up and down, and, on examination, thought
I should like her. She was a tall woman, five
feet seven inches—I know that, as I measured
her lots of times afterwards — her eyes were
blue, and she had beautiful dark hair all in
ringlets, which seemed to me splendid. As
was the fashion then, she had a great hoop
round her, a crinoline.

"I suppose you could eat a bit of something
this morning," she said.

"Thank you, miss," I replied.

So she went out into the pantry, cut me
off a beef-steak, grilled it, and roasted some
potatoes. That done, she took a cup, drew
a pint of cider, and placed a chair for me.
Quite a feast! I thought, "If this is the way
you are going on, you'll find me here pretty
often. Such a good maid!"

Then we got into conversation. She asked
me whether I was married.

"Married? No. Sure enough, I am not
married," I said.

"Oh, I didn't know," she answered. "You
can't depend on strangers. I didn't know

whether you were married or not, or had got a young woman."

Next she inquired how old I was.

"Thirty," I said.

"You don't look thirty," she replied. "I consider, if that's your age, you've been about a long time not to have had a young woman."

("Ah!" I thought, "you mustn't know all, or I shan't have any beef, or yet cider.")

"I suppose you go to church on Sundays?" she queried.

"Well, really," I said, "that's my busiest day, the time when most of the poaching's done. Perhaps I might be able to come down Sunday evenings."

After that I used to call nearly every day, and Susan gave me a drink of cider, as well as something to eat—usually bread and cheese. My forenoons having been provided for, I thought I must look out a place for my afternoons. So, as I went about, I called at the people's houses and made myself pretty sociable. Amongst other places, I knocked at the door of a dairy, where there was an old man, an old woman, and a young woman who, I thought, looked at me.

I CHANGE MY CALLING

"Are you a fresh man, just come here?" asked the old man.

"Yes," I answered.

"Oh, well," he said, "I hope you'll get on. You'll have a very good master."

As he spoke, I observed the young woman casting her eyes upon me again. Soon after, the old people went out to serve the pigs or calves, or some such business. As soon as they were gone, I turned to the young woman and asked her what she was.

"Are you a servant?" I said.

"No," she replied; "I'm a daughter."

"Not married?"

"Lor', no!" she said.

"Nor yet engaged?"

"Oh, no!—no!" she answered, firmly.

"Well," I said, "I'm on the lookout." (I had just come from the other place, down below.)

"Then you're in the same case as myself," she replied, looking pleased. "You had better sit down. Father and mother will be in directly, and will ask you to drink."

"I suppose your father and mother are always at home?" I suggested.

"Oh, no!" she answered: "father goes calf-jobbing nearly every day, and father and mother always go to market on Saturdays."

I took this as a hint, and when Saturday came, duly put in an appearance. Nobody was there but the daughter.

"Will you take something to eat?" she inquired. ("Good!" I thought. "Living won't cost me much at this rate. Two places already.")

"Thank you," I replied.

"Do you like eggs?"

"Oh yes." I may mention that "forenoons" are a regular institution in Devonshire. The habit is not so common at Dulverton.

Betsy put the frying-pan on the fire, cut up some streaky bacon, laid the rashers in the pan, and when the bacon was fried, took five or six eggs from the table, broke them into the pan, stirred them until they became what is called "scrambled," and then I had a jolly blow out. Of course, she did not forget to draw me some cider.

After I had eaten as much as I was inclined to, I began to take stock of her. She was short, good on her legs, and had light hair and grey eyes.

"Not so good as t'other one," I thought to

178

myself. "Do to find me in grub, but, as regards courting, I don't know so much about that." However, I had to tell her that I loved her, or I should not have fared so well.

When Sunday evening came, I went back to the first. Nobody was there, save the lady herself, pretty, gay, and smart. A dress-maker was Susan, and wore silk dresses. I, too, was arrayed in my best, and she at once ran her eye over me.

"I don't like your clothes at all," she said.

"Why?" asked I.

"Oh, they ain't the fashion," she answered.

"What's wrong with them?" I inquired again.

"Well, I should like to see you with a good frock coat and a box hat."

"Yes, yes," I thought, "but they would cost money." I hinted as much.

"Oh," she said, "but you must have them, and I don't much admire your shirt for Sundays. Here's a fair offer. If you'll get the coat and hat, I'll make you the shirt."

I was not particularly well off for money, but, in obedience to her wishes, I went into Honiton and ordered the articles. On re-

179

ceiving them from the tailor, I paid her another visit.

"That's more like it," she said approvingly. "Now I shall be able to go out with you." She, on her part, presented me with the shirt, which was all plaited about the front, and I gave her a kiss or two extra for it. Enough to make one to, wasn't it?

Meanwhile, I kept the old rules with the other girl, and, after a time, she began to inquire whether I should like to get married.

"Oh, I don't know," I replied carelessly, "I am in no hurry about that yet." Whereupon, if the old man and her mother were away, she would give me some whiskey. At length I would wish her good-bye, saying, "See you again to-morrow, Betsy."

On my next visit to Susan, *she* wanted to know when I was going to get married.

"Any time will do," I replied. Meanwhile, to make matters still worse, I was writing home to a Dulverton girl, who ultimately became my wife. However, Susan kept pestering me on the subject until I agreed to go to Exeter with her, and have the knot tied. I wrote to my brother, a gamekeeper at Lady Rolle's, asking him to meet us at

I CHANGE MY CALLING

Exeter, and there we called at a registrar's. To our amazement and dismay we found that the ceremony could not take place until we had stayed in the city—slept there—so many nights. On hearing this, we went home again. In spite of disappointment, Susan did not let the idea drop, but kept on with me about marrying, though she did not want her father to be informed, exactly. We talked the matter over and over, and at last decided that we would be married in the workhouse at Honiton. I went into the town, paid down seven shillings, and was assured that the banns should be hung up. The wedding was seemingly in sight, but, on the eve of the marriage, Susan was taken ill. She proved to be in a galloping consumption, and soon, very soon, the poor thing died. Barring this misfortune, I should have had her—there is no question of that.

After the funeral, I went back to the scrambled eggs, which, indeed, I had never forsaken. Betsy was in profound ignorance of what had occurred, and of my relations with poor Susan, so I found no difficulty in following on there for a time. I then heard that Mr Barne—he was the rector of our

church at Combe Raleigh—had a fine lot of
maidens at his house, so I used to go up and
have a little larking with them, while they
helped me to cider. One day, when I called,
the old gentleman was away, but, as it turned
out, not very far off. The girls told me that
they were going to take up an upstairs carpet
—would I help it down with them? There
could be only one reply—to place my services
at their disposal.

By-and-by we heard a rat-tat at the door.
"'Tis master!" they sang out, upon which
I rambled and scrambled down the stairs
faster than ever I went up, and, on reaching
the bottom, bolted out at the back door. In
my haste and excitement I left my gun behind. As soon as I missed it, I became
anxious, and thought to myself, "However am
I to get my gun? Perhaps the old man will
see it." Then it occurred to me that he had
glebe land, and that I was supposed to kill
rabbits for him. So, without more ado, I
returned to the house, and knocking at the
door, just as if I had never been there, asked
to see Mr Barne. One of the maidens handed
me the gun, and when the old gentleman came
out into the hall, I could not have presented

a different appearance if I had but just arrived. On seeing him, I said:

"Please, sir, when do you want a couple of rabbits?"

"Oh, any time the latter end of the week," he replied. "Cook, draw Holcombe some cider."

"Then," I thought, "I've slipped through this all right."

The same night a similar incident occurred, which, however, ended otherwise. There used to work for us a little bit of a fellow called Spider, a painter, who, like myself, used to slink up there after work-time, and have a spree with the maidens. They went on with their games to such degree, that the old gentleman, who was in his study, heard them, and walked downstairs to learn the meaning of the disturbance. The maidens heard him coming, and, without a moment's hesitation popped little Spider in the cupboard, and fastened the cupboard door. When Mr Barne entered, he found nobody but the servants. However, he was full of suspicions. Perhaps the girls' looks betrayed them, perhaps he had heard something go snick. Anyhow, he stepped straight across to the cupboard door, and was in the act of opening it, when out jumped Spider, who ran between the parson's legs, almost knocking him down, and away to the hall door, leaving his hat behind. The old gentleman, in a pretty rage, asked whom he came to see. One said one, another another, but at last they fixed on one, and she got the sack.

With regard to little Spider, I remember being told that he and a mason, who was a heavy drinker, went on one occasion to Chard. There they spent all their money except just enough to enable one of them to return by train. So the old mason proposed to Spider that he should be tied up in a sack. He was to lie out stiff and not move, as if he were a bundle of laths, and in that way it was hoped that he might be smuggled through without paying his fare. Spider agreed, and his companion, having tied him up in the sack, carried him down to the station, and threw him under the seat in the railway carriage. Porters and guard were completely deceived, and when the pair reached Honiton, Spider was pulled out, and the mason bore him from the station under his arm. Nothing could have been more successful.

I CHANGE MY CALLING

To return to my love affairs. I did not desert Betsy; indeed, I was more regular in my attendance than ever, availing myself of every chance to partake of her bacon and eggs. But still I was not satisfied, and, after I had been going there a good bit, thought I must look out another place. I called at a fresh dairy-house, where I found a woman. She was alone, and asked me to take some cider. After I had drained a cup, I inquired if she was married.

"Yes," she replied, "I am—more's the pity!"

"Why?" said I.

"Because I don't like my husband," was the answer, "I was taken in."

Thereupon I wished her good-bye or good-day, when, to my surprise, she called after me,

"Be sure you call in any time you are passing, and have a drink."

"Funny woman!" I thought, but, if I was near the spot, I generally stopped and drank, and after a while she began to give me something to eat as well. Then I reflected that matters were getting warm.

"You are surely falling in love with me," said I to myself. "I shall chuck this, or you will be murdering your husband."

Accordingly, I put an end to the game.

Soon after this Club day came round—a great day at Combe Raleigh. All the parish must go to the club walk, and there I fell in with Betsy. After the proceedings were over, I kept her out all night, and the circumstance got to her father's ears. Of course, he was very angry, and declared he would shoot me if he caught me at his house again. Neither the old man nor the old woman knew that I was courting the maid, but, supposing that I called out of friendship, had received me cordially, and many a time we had all sat for hours playing cards. This was now to stop. The old couple wished their daughter to marry somebody who had money. They knew that I was a larking sort of fellow, and, as for money, they did not consider that I had any.

Close by their cottage ran a road, which I had often to use in the course of my duty. One day I was passing when out ran Betsy. She told me that her father and mother were out, and repeated all that he had said about shooting me, but advised me to pay no heed to his threats, and come on Saturdays, as before, whilst they were at market. So I kept up my Saturday visits, with their pleasant accompani-

I CHANGE MY CALLING

ment of bacon and eggs, for, I should think, two or three years. Well, then I got married. Before taking this step, I informed my master, and pointing out that a house was vacant, inquired whether it would suit him to let me have it. Mr Barnett was very kind, and most readily assented. Moreover, he put the house in thorough repair, and made a nice cottage of it. My wife's name was Ann Chilcott. She was a Dulverton woman, and liked me before I went game-keeping, but she had no connection with the poaching gang. After we were married we enjoyed much happiness and got on very well together.

Returning to other matters. It was Christmas time, and I had been spending the evening at a farmhouse, playing cards with Mr Broom, a dairyman. On my way home I heard a shot fired. I immediately went back, and called a man employed by Mr Barnett.

"Get up," I said, "and come with me. There's some poaching going on."

"I can't," he replied, "I'm very tired."

As I had my gun with me, I did not trouble him further and proceeded in the direction from which the sound had come. Soon after I heard another shot. By this time I was thoroughly

187

familiar with the neighbourhood, and decided to "head them off," by getting into a wood which I made sure they would visit.

I was not deceived. Through the wood ran a wheel-path used for removing timber, and close by the path stood a tree on which was a hen-pheasant. I had hardly time to notice this when I heard another shot at the bottom of that very wood. I got under some bushes, hid away as best I could, and waited. Soon I heard them coming. They saw the pheasant, shot at it, and, as it happened, winged it. When, however, they came to look, they found it a difficult matter to find the bird. After running about for some time, they gave up the search and were moving away up the path, when I jumped out.

I was pretty close to them, and the man who had the gun, put it to his shoulder, and pointed it at me. In reply, I put my gun to my shoulder, pointed it at them, and told them to stand. I knew *their* gun wasn't loaded, as it had been just fired. I then went up to the men, and identified them. The land on which they were trespassing belonged, not to Mr Barnett, but to Squire Worth. It became necessary for me, therefore, to proceed to

I CHANGE MY CALLING

Worth House, near Tiverton, and see the gentleman.

" I am very glad you have caught 'em," he said, "and shall feel obliged to you, Holcombe, if you'll take out a summons. Meanwhile, here's a sovereign for you."

I obeyed his instructions, and in due course the trespassers appeared before the magistrates, who awarded them three months each. One of them, a mason, and a proper, fine, upstanding man who might have tied me to a tree and left me to starve, had said that no man, whether watcher or keeper, should ever take him or his companions. To show his appreciation of my skill and courage in tackling these old, bold, experienced poachers my master presented me with half-a-sovereign, to which a gentleman at Lipput, called Blake, was good enough to add five shillings. Most extraordinary of all, I saw the mason's wife several times afterwards, and she was ready to treat me to anything. She declared it was the best day's work I ever did in my life, as it sobered her husband, and led to his becoming more steady.

I had a good master in Mr Barnett, who allowed me to give rabbits to the men, thus encouraging them to preserve the game. I did my best also to keep the farmers pleased, but my efforts in this direction were impeded by a considerable difficulty. They had no special reason to oblige me, and they had the great advantage of being able to destroy game without anything becoming known—*i.e.* by treading nests. However, as I have said, pheasants and partridges continued to increase until the coverts were well-stocked.

I was out one day when I saw a man trying a hedge with a dog and gun. Going round very quietly, I walked up to him and asked him what he was about.

"Only just passing," he replied.

"Very funny!" I observed, "but I must have your gun."

I was about to take it from him, when, before I realised his intention, he laid hold of me and threw me on my back. The next moment he was gone, and I saw no more of him. However, I knew the man, and knew his name. Accordingly, I said to my master, "I wish to take out a summons against him, sir."

Mr Barnett was agreeable, but, when an attempt was made to serve the summons, it was found that the culprit had left the country and fled to America, whence he never returned. He was a moderately tall and terribly "stiff-grown" fellow, belonging to Lipput. Whether I should have had any chance with him, if he had not taken me unawares, I can hardly say, but, of course, many a good laugh was raised at my expense, especially at Combe Raleigh. My master, on the other hand, tried to comfort me.

"Never mind," he said, "as long as he's out of the country. He won't kill any more game."

I am conscious that my achievements as gamekeeper pale in comparison with what I did in my poaching days, but it is well known to people experienced in such matters that opportunities for bringing off a *coup* are decidedly rare, and many gamekeepers, trusted and respected by their employers, cannot boast of a single capture. This must be my excuse for mentioning a little incident which might otherwise not be worth recording. It was winter, and myself and two men, who used to accompany me were out watching. By-and-by we heard a rabbit cry. Going forward, we found a rabbit caught in a gin. We lay still and waited till the morning. Somewhere about eight o'clock, our friend turned up, and was detained whilst we searched the hedge. A great many traps were discovered, and, of course, confiscated. We knew the man, and forwarded his name to Mr Barnett, at Morebath House. He was summoned before the magistrates, who offered him the alternative of a fine or a month's imprisonment. He paid.

Not long after, my master became unwell. He removed from Morebath to Ottery St Mary, hoping that he might benefit by the change, but, as he did not improve, sent for me, and said,

"Holcombe, I am very bad, and fear I shall not be able to shoot next season, so I have decided to let the place to Major Warry, who will no doubt be glad of your services."

I felt very sorry, and, having expressed regret, went back to my duties. It happened that we had a farmer who went out rabbiting a good deal. In fact, he was out nearly every day. I informed Major Warry, who told me to watch him and take the rabbits away. In obedience to these instructions, I watched them—a farmer and a dairyman—but made no attempt to interfere until night, when they finished off. I then approached them with the remark that I had orders to take the rabbits.

"Who authorised you?" they asked.

"Major Warry," I replied. "Mr Barnett is bad, and he has the shooting."

They gave up the rabbits. I had encountered them on a furze brake, full of burrows, so I was not surprised to find, on opening the bag, as many as thirty-two rabbits. I carried them home to Major Warry, who gave them all to poor people in the village and "about to go." After that, the farmers took against him. The report was carried into Honiton town and all round the country, and it was decided on the Fifth of November to burn him.

On gunpowder day a proper gang came out from Honiton. Altogether there were several hundreds, some of them dressed in old rabbit-skins, others with rabbit-skins on poles, and a barrel of beer was rolled up on the lawn. It was impossible to recognise them as they had blacked their faces, or wore masks, and for a long time they kept up a fine game, screeching, howling, letting off fire-works, and the like. As for me, I remained indoors, or I might perhaps have been killed.

AUTOBIOGRAPHY OF A POACHER

Well, when they had burned the Major's image, and had their fill of drinking and excitement at the mansion, they came to my house. There they burnt me, and almost set fire to my cottage. The gate was burnt outright, and the door singed. It was a proper keeper's cottage with a thatched roof, so that I had good reason to be alarmed. Afterwards, when it was almost too late, I had it insured. Major Warry did not remain long unpopular. He was a very nice man, and, when he came to understand matters, all became friendly again.

This episode occurred before the Ground Game Act was passed, and both masters and keepers found it hard work to please the farmers. Speaking as a gamekeeper, I don't thank Mr Gladstone for passing that Act. I am not opposed to farmers keeping rabbits down, but see how the poor hares have suffered! Where there is now one hare there used to be fifty. And hares I consider tip-top game. In my poaching days I have killed hares in all the parishes round here,— Dulverton, Anstey, Hawkridge, Withypool, Exford, Winsford, King's Brompton, Lux-borough, Treborough, Carhampton, Brendon

I CHANGE MY CALLING

Hill, Withiel Florey, Skilgate, Upton, Exton, Morebath, Bampton, Stoodleigh, Oakford, and Brushford.

However, I don't want to discuss that now, but to show how I suffered as a gamekeeper, in my attempts to please farmers. One of our Combe Raleigh farmers had a brother who, he told me, was coming down from London, and would I allow him to go out rabbiting with me?

"Yes," I said, "he can go out."

When the brother arrived, I was reminded of my promise, and made an appointment accordingly. We had killed two or three rabbits between us when we came to a pit covered with brambles.

"There's sure to be a rabbit in there," I said. "I'll go over to that gate, and turn the rabbit towards you, so that you may have a shot."

The manœuvre succeeded; the rabbit came out. Instead of shooting the rabbit, however, my companion shot me, pointing his gun straight at me. One of the shot made a dent in my watch which necessitated my having it beaten out. The other nine-and-twenty lodged in my person, not a few of them in my head.

I was taken to a doctor who extracted some of the intruders, and to whom I remarked that it was harder to get them out than to put them in. He laughed. The process was so troublesome that it was thought advisable to leave the shot in their beds, and there they are now, a great many of them.

CHAPTER VIII

I CONTINUE KEEPERING

ALTHOUGH I was not successful in catching many poachers at Honiton, I cannot reproach myself with any lack of zeal. Indeed, I was too zealous, as the following incident will show. At Combe Raleigh there was a copse, in which I heard shots fired, as it were, in and out—perhaps once a fortnight; but, in spite of all my efforts, I failed to discover the culprit. At last I thought I would set a trap and see if I could catch him. It happened that I had an old hogshead, which had been used for cider, and was now almost worn out. So one day I took a shovel, a digger—either a pick-axe or a "bisgay"; I can't remember which—and a wheel-barrow, and went up to a spot in the wood where two shooting paths met, a four-cross-way. Here I started digging; and although it took a long time, I did not stop until I had "sunk" out of the middle of the cross-way a great hole large enough to contain the barrel. Meanwhile I carted away the soil in the wheel-barrow; otherwise the offenders might have seen it, and perhaps suspected the design. Then I let down the hogshead, which I filled with water from an old pond hard by. My next step was to lay some nice dry sticks over the mouth of the barrel; and on the sticks I placed a coat of moss resembling the rest of the path, so that it was impossible to distinguish anything.

All that remained now was to watch the result, and every morning I went up to see if anybody was in the hogshead, or had been in it. No such luck! I was regularly disappointed, until at last I came almost to forget the existence of the barrel, and certainly gave up all expectation of success. Well, one day I had been out with a party of farmers rabbiting, and, I suppose I must admit, had taken a little drop too much cider. On my way back—I nearly always used that path in returning home—I thought nothing about the trap I had set, and popped right into it, with both feet—bang! I was up to my waist in water, and frightened just to death. But in a sense the shock did me good, for I was a bit drunkish, and that made me fresh. Having scrambled out, I steered away home to the old woman, who, seeing me drenched and filthy, asked me where I had been to get in that mess. At first I didn't care to say, as I knew I should catch it. However, she pressed me, and at last I blurted out the truth.

"Well!" she exclaimed, "that's just as it should be. Nothing could be better. You know you used to be a poacher yourself, and you had no business to attempt such things."

I begged her not to tell anybody of my adventure, and I believe she never did, but for a long while — who can blame her?— she used to tease me about the hogshead. I should add that, to prevent similar occurrences in the future, the next morning I went and dug up the old barrel, broke it to pieces, and filled in the hole with the earth I had wheeled away. Isn't there a passage in Scripture about a person falling into a pit that he had dug for others? I fancy I have read it, and, as you have seen, it was fully exemplified in my own case.

One day, in the latter part of September, Major Warry and I were out looking over the grounds, in order to observe if there were any birds about, and we came to a stubble-field. On reaching the gate, I noticed a figure at the bottom of the field, and, turning to Major Warry, remarked,

"There's a man down there."

"Yes," he replied, "I see there is. Go where he will, you follow him and catch him."

I set off, but the fellow apparently did not think he was doing much. At all events, he did not move until I was within gunshot. Then he took to his heels. Away he fled, out by Langford Bridge, I after him, and straight towards Honiton. He kept well in front, dashed right into the town, and down through the town, while people stared and wondered what was up, and at last he took refuge in a lodging-house. I was pretty close to him when he gained the door, and pursued him up the stairs, and into a bedroom, where I found him sitting on a chair. I had fairly run him to earth.

I was about to accost him, when I turned my eye round, and saw a black man or black woman in bed. I cannot swear to the sex; at any rate, it was a black face. Undisturbed by this circumstance, I demanded my friend's name. He gave it like a man, — "William

Sweetland." On hearing who he was, I twigged him as a proper sort of hand for the job. I had never come in contact with Sweetland, but he was notorious for getting about from place to place—poaching, of course—and nobody could catch him.

Having concluded my business, I went downstairs. At the bottom I found the landlord, brandishing his stick. He was hoarse with rage, and anxious to learn by what authority I had entered his house.

"Oh!" I said, "I had orders."

After a bustle I managed to get out, of which I was very glad, for at one time he seemed inclined to lock the door on me. Going up the street I met the major on his way down. I told him what had happened, and he asked me whether I knew the fellow. I answered, "Yes," and we proceeded to call on Mr Stamp, the lawyer. The latter inquired what we had seen. We informed him, whereupon he observed,

"I don't see what you can do in it, unless you have the man up for trespass, and that won't be worth the trouble. As for you, Holcombe," he added, winking at me, "you may think yourself lucky if they don't have *you* up for invading another man's premises."

However, as we took no steps, they thought it better to let the matter blow over.

At the end of the season Major Warry left, and about the same time, to my deep sorrow, my master, Mr Barnett, died. He was a good master—as good as gold. Indeed, I cannot imagine a better. His eldest son, Mr Henry Barnett, was in the army, and, on his father's death, he succeeded to the property. During his short reign nothing particular happened, so far as I was concerned. My new master was fond of shooting, and it was often my duty to accompany him. One day we were out, when he complained of being unwell.

"Well, sir," I said, "let's go home."

"No," he replied, "go on a little further."

At last, however, he was obliged to give up. He went home, took to his bed. In a week the poor man was dead, and I had lost another good master. The next heir, the present Mr Barnett, went through the Ashantee War—that which took place in King Coffee's time; and, on his return, there were great rejoicings. For some space I continued to serve this gentleman, and found him a good master. Then a little misunderstanding arose, and I decided to seek another place. Glancing

I CONTINUE KEEPERING

through the papers, I saw that Sir John Shelley, of Shobrook Park, Crediton, wanted a keeper. I applied. Sir John replied asking whether I could furnish satisfactory references, and I gave the name of Mr Arthur Barnett, who, I believed, would satisfy him. As a matter of fact, I applied for and obtained the situation before I acquainted Mr Barnett with my intention of leaving. However, it turned out all right. Directly the affair was settled, I gave a month's notice.

"What are you going for?" asked Mr Barnett.

"No particular reason, sir," I answered, "but I think it time that I had a change."

"Very well," he said.

This occurred in September, and Mr Barnett, wishing to retain my services to the end of October, wrote to Sir John Shelley requesting him to say whether it would make any difference. The answer was — "No; you can keep him on, if you wish." That alone will show that I was not so badly beloved. But I can bring forward other proofs. Mr Barnett gave me a good character, and, when I asked him for a copy, was obliging enough to write one out and hand it to me. Amongst other things in this testimonial I noticed the expressions "sober" and "honest." With regard to soberness, it is the sad truth that I was drunk seven months out of the twelve; and, as for honesty, 'twas I first, and master next. That is the way of keepers. Altogether I was with the Barnetts fourteen years, and they were splendid masters, all three.

At the end of October we packed off to Yeoford Junction, where my beat lay. I made a good start, caught a man wiring, and got on fairly well during the season. I then told Sir John Shelley that I was accustomed to have a week's holiday, and he granted me the same privilege. Accordingly, I came home for the club-walk. When I got to Dulverton, I found my mother-in-law ill, and over-stayed my time. Perhaps Sir John's steward thought this illness a pretext; at all events, on my return to Crediton, Mr Smith appeared dissatisfied, and gave me a month's notice. I did not like that summary style of dismissal, as the steward soon learnt.

"I don't know about going at the end of the month," I said. "I shall go when I can get a place."

As a matter of fact, I stayed on for two

months, but, of course, under the circumstances
I could not regard the post as a permanency.
After a while I heard of a place at Arlington
Court, near Barnstaple, the seat of Sir Bruce
Chichester, and was engaged. On inquiry I
was told that my work would consist very
largely in stopping rabbit-holes by day and
using long nets by night. As some people
may read this book who do not understand
sport I may explain what is meant by the
latter operation. At night rabbits go out to
feed. If the moon is up, or there is sufficient
light to see what you are about, you take out
long nets and fix them up in a perpendicular
position between the rabbits and their runs.
You now go round to the rear, and turn the
rabbits in the direction of the nets. The result
is that they get entangled, like fish, and you
often secure a good haul. This is not a bad
way of keeping rabbits down, and farmers and
others may no doubt find it very useful. At
Dulverton, in my poaching days, I had adopted
the plan myself, but I did not feel that it was
proper work for a gamekeeper.

I should add that this netting was the pretext
for a good deal of merriment. The butler and
a whole lot of people came out, and, of course,

we drank each other's healths. However, that did not alter my dislike of the place, which was in more than one sense uncongenial. For instance, Sir Bruce sent away all his rabbits. No doubt he had a right to do what he liked with his own, but I did not approve of the practice and abused my position, as some might say, by gratifying his tenants at his expense. One day I was returning with the trapper, both laden with rabbits, when we came to a farm-house. I told the young man what I proposed doing, upon which he exclaimed,

"What about the head-keeper?"

"You needn't mind him," I replied, "but if you're afraid, stand outside and keep watch."

I then knocked at the door, and said to the farmer's wife,

"If you please, ma'am, here are a brace of rabbits for you, if you will accept them."

"Thank you, kindly," she replied, "a brace of rabbits will be quite a treat."

Not content with this acknowledgment she called us both in, refreshed us with a quart of beer apiece, and gave us each a hot cake just out of the oven.

"There!" said I, turning to Jim, "that's what comes of doing people a kindness."

I CONTINUE KEEPERING

Hardly had we left the house when we saw the head-keeper approaching. He was a little suspicious, and asked us what we had been doing so long. We kept our own counsel, however, and, so far as that matter was concerned, nothing leaked out.

The next morning I got acting the same part at another farmhouse, and I fancy the old man must have smelt a rat. At all events, after I had given the woman the rabbits and drank her cider, of which I was very glad, I went outside, and there met the head-keeper. He had come to meet me again.

"What were you about in there?" he inquired.

"Carried the farmer a brace of rabbits."

"You've no right to do that. Go in and fetch 'em out again."

"Not I!" I answered. "You can fetch 'em out yourself."

But he didn't. It may have been unjust, but I had my doubts about that keeper. The rabbits were always packed the first thing in the morning. However, I did not leave on his account, but because I was not used to carrying seven dozen of traps on my back, and being out with the long nets three nights a week.

AUTOBIOGRAPHY OF A POACHER

Just now I mentioned Jim Comer, my assistant. He had a remarkable appetite, that boy, and could eat three full-grown rabbits a day. Even that, however, was nothing to what happened a few months later at Newton Abbott. I know there eight fellows who made a bet that they would go to Totnes and eat sixteen pounds of beef. Accordingly they set off, and, repairing to an inn, had their sixteen pounds cooked, cleared that, and asked the landlord for eight pounds more. Cleared that, and when the landlord appeared again, called for yet more, whereupon the publican exclaimed,

"Eat the plates, you beggars!"

The feasters returned to Newton, full to repletion, and those who bet against them paid for the grub.

At the expiration of the month I went back to my wife at Yeoford. Mr Smith came to see me.

"So you're not gone yet, Holcombe," he said.

"No, sir," I said, "and I don't mean to until I can get a permanent place. You put me in here, but you did not tell me when I was to go out again."

However, it was not long before I heard of a place at Newton Abbot, under Mr William Vicary, the tanner. I sent in an application,

I CONTINUE KEEPERING

and was successful. We now removed our things to Newton Abbot, leaving Mr Smith in peace, and I daresay that gentleman was glad to be quit of us. Mr Vicary was a very good master. He had not a great deal of land, and my principal occupation was feeding. Mr Vicary did not stint me; I had loads of corn. The place, I forgot to say, was called Netherton, and Mr Vicary's rights took in Milvern Hill. It was a fine bit of shooting.

I remained at Newton Abbot for a couple of years, and during that time had a fresh experience of Cockney sportsmanship. A neighbouring farmer had invited two friends down from London, and we all went out rabbiting together. We particularly cautioned the visitors, "Whatever you do, on no account shoot at the comb of the hedge." It so happened that the very first rabbit that came out got on the top of the hedge, and one of the London fellows blazed at it. I was on the other side of the fence and so was once more a victim. As on the previous occasion, I received the shot in my head, and a man standing beside me made up his mind that I was dead. They carried me home, put me to bed, and sent for the doctor.

The medico arrived, bandaged up my head as well as he could, but for several days could not stop the bleeding. He then said that he had arranged with another doctor to come and take out the shot. Accordingly, they cut open my head and extracted some, but for many months I lay by and failed to recover my health. I found that my head began to shake a little, as they predicted it would, and it has shaken ever since.

It seems that a shot has got on one of the nerves, and this shot no doctor—I have tried several—will undertake to remove. It is, there is no need to say, an exceedingly unpleasant affliction, though, happily, not painful. To make things still better, Mr Vicary sent to inform me that he intended to give up the shooting. Thus, you see, I was in a fix. As soon as I was well enough, I called on my master and asked who was going to pay for all this doctoring and expense.

"The man that shot you, Holcombe," he answered.

Mr Vicary put himself to a good deal of trouble in ascertaining the name of the person, where he came from, and other matters of the kind, and when he had obtained sufficient information entered a claim on my behalf for twenty pounds,

I CONTINUE KEEPERING

with an intimation that, if the money were not paid by a certain time, the claim would be doubled. The doctor's bill was already settled, and within a month the money required for compensation also arrived. After that I was out for twelve months knocking about with a man that went to Torquay, selling eggs, butter, poultry, and apples.

My next experiment in game-keeping was somewhat of a novelty. I saw an advertisement stating that a man was wanted to attend two gentlemen and assist in killing game for the season. The address was East Down, about seven miles from Barnstaple. I called, and was considerably surprised to learn that the two gentlemen were deaf and dumb. The real master was called Cardis, while the other's name was Dickinson. The arrangements were made through the missus, who worked the deaf and dumb alphabet in talking to the gentlemen, and she it was who informed me when they proposed to go out. I stayed with them during the season, and, naturally, my experiences were rather funny. They would walk on one side of the hedge, and I on the other; and when they came to a good bed of holes, they would raise their guns as a signal to me to stop and try the earths.

AUTOBIOGRAPHY OF A POACHER

It was always our rule to carry a spade with us, to be used in case of need. If the ferret lay up they would motion to me to listen. If I heard anything, we immediately set ourselves to dig him up and spit him out. When we had recovered the ferret, we would go on and stick to it all day. Another time we might shoot pheasants, or partridges. If I shot well, Cardis would hold up his thumb to signify "Good!" I used to kill more than both the others put together, and, in fact, at this stage of my career was apparently a gentleman-killer rather than keeper. On the whole I found them very tidy men, but did not remain long with them. In fact, at the end of the season for which I was hired, I left.

After quiting the deaf and dumb gentlemen, I was out of a place for a good bit. As I was married and had become used to regular work, this was a state of things I could not regard with satisfaction. I therefore took train to Totnes and called on Mr Oldroyd, a lawyer and land-agent. To him I unfolded my wishes, whereupon he inquired about references. There was no difficulty here, as I always carried my "characters" in my pocket. He put down my name and address, and said he would let me know if he heard anything. Even then quite three months elapsed before I received a message from him. However, at last he sent to Netherton, where I had been living all this while, and desired me to attend at his office. I went and he told me that a place was vacant at Buckland-in-the Moor, Mr Bastard's estate, near Ashburton. He mentioned the wages offered, etc., and we soon came to terms. Mr Buckland proved an excellent master, and I stayed with him two years. He, however, had another place— Kidley, near Yealmpton, Plymouth, and on his giving up the Buckland establishment, I was obliged to leave. My tenure of this post was not marked by any exploits that I know of. The chief circumstance connected with Buckland was the tremendous plague of rabbits, to which there was literally no end, and I and a chap that served under me found constant employment in killing them.

On our leaving Dartmoor I recollect my wife saying to me,

"What are you going to perform now?"

"I've thought of taking a public-house," I answered.

"Then," said she, "you must keep pigs."

"Well, I suppose we must keep some pigs,"

I replied, "but what do you mean? What have pigs to do with a public-house?"

"Why, to eat the grains," she answered, "you can be depended on to drink all the syrup that comes from them." Publicans, of course, brewed their own beer in those days, but it was brewed to sell. The project fell through.

Then, we sold up, and, hiring a pony and trap, I drove my wife, first to Exeter, where we stayed one night, and then to Battleton, my wife's home at Dulverton. For some time I had nothing to do. One morning, however, I took it into my head to walk to Exeter and wait upon Mr Edmund Snow. I was well known to this gentleman, as he used to come over to Honiton shooting, and I thought it possible that he might be willing, and able, to help me. He received me kindly.

"Well, Holcombe, what do you want with me?"

"If you please, sir," I replied, "do you know of a gamekeeper's place?"

He considered for a moment, and then answered, "No, I don't, but I will tell you what I do know. The conservators intend to place a water-bailiff on the river—where, I cannot say. If you think the appointment suitable, I will

write you a note, which you may take to
Mr Walkey."

As it seemed at the moment the only thing
to do, I consented, took the note to Mr
Walkey, and, after meeting him at Mr Ford's
office, agreed to watch the river here at
Dulverton. So things went on, in and out,
for a couple of years. Whatever attractions
this job had for me—and of course, it was very
pleasant to be back at Dulverton, and among
old friends—it had one fatal objection. I
mean, it was not permanent. When therefore
Mr Newbury, who lived in a neighbouring
mansion,—Combe,—was said to be wanting
a man who would go to Wales, I had no hesitation in applying for the place. I was fortunate,
and got it. Mr Newbury rented a house and
shooting at Bringlas Hall near Welshpool in
North Wales, and thither I accompanied him,
leaving my wife at home. It was a late country,
and the partridges got into the standing corn
pretty much. Accordingly Mr Newbury would
send me into the fields to "rise" the birds. I
not only "rose," but shot at them, always with
his consent, and thus helped to kill the game.

However, our ways did not please everybody.
An old Welsh farmer, or his wife, would come

out gabbling and gabbling away—presumably, about our treading down the corn. I neither could nor would understand them, for, after making signs to them, I used to go amongst the corn again. Then we would proceed to another farm, where the same thing would happen. In answer to their protests, I always said in good Somerset—"I don't knaw what you be telling about." If I wanted to buy a fowl from any of these old farmers, I was compelled to show them the money and point.

Mr Newbury got lodgings for me, and 'twas the funniest place I ever was at in my life. The people could not understand English, and when the time came to go to bed, the old woman put a rush into the pan, and fried it with fat. Before I was half undressed, the rush was out. I was obliged to tell Mr Newbury that I could not stand it. He then procured lodgings for me in the village, — at Lanvaer,— with the understanding that I was to come to the house for meat and drink. We remained in North Wales for twelve months, and during that time killed up most of the stuff there was about.

I remember Mr Newbury addressed a letter to Sir Watkins Wynn asking permission to fish

I CONTINUE KEEPERING

in his river. I can't tell the name of the river, and, if I could, should probably spell it wrong, like the rest of these crack-jaw words. It was very private water. However, Mr Newbury obtained leave, and one morning he and I set off for a long tramp of seven miles. Our labour was not wasted, for that day we caught so many fish that we got fairly sick and decided not to take any more. (Of course, I refer to fly-fishing.) On the other hand, when we tried the Severn, we did nothing. From this you will perceive what a difference it makes when water is preserved. At the close of the season, Mr Newbury took another place—Sheepwash, Black Torrington ; and I came home to see my wife. The latter had heard that, if I cared to accept, I might have a permanent place and regular employment as water-bailiff at Dulverton. As this opening suited me better, I communicated with Mr Newbury, and informed him I had resolved to take the water-job again.

Before I describe my experiences on the river, there are a good many little matters to which I should like to refer in connection with my career both as poacher and gamekeeper. First, about guns. In the course of my life I have gone out with dozens of gentlemen shooting, and, amongst

other things, have observed that the bad shots
were never without an excuse. The fault was
always in the gun. Either it was too straight in
the stock, or it was too crooked—or, perhaps, it
was top-heavy. Now, in all these cases it is my
belief that the real culprit was, not the gun, but
what was behind the gun. I am led to entertain
this opinion the more strongly on account of
what I have myself accomplished.

I have used all manner of guns, from an old
flint-lock to a she, or hammerless, gun, and
found I could shoot with any of them. I will
even go so far as to say that, if I had a common
stick, and a nipple were put to it, I could shoot
with that. I have killed seven partridges at
one shot. I have thrown shot from a muzzle-
loader through a penny piece. Not a man in
Dulverton could do that, as he would not know
how. If I wanted a double charge for any
purpose—such as killing a horse or bullock,
which farmers would give me when used up,
for the dogs—I cut a cork so as to match it
between the two triggers, pulled, and the two
barrels went off at once. I heard a few days
ago that my poor old gun, that has shed so
much blood, is living yet, and I should dearly
love to see it.

I CONTINUE KEEPERING

To resume—I have shot a wood-cock perched on the limb of a tree. Such a thing, I suppose, has never been known in the age of man. The bird must have been wounded. I have caught two rabbits in a single gin, and two in a single net. One morning, whilst I was at Honiton, I was going up beside the river Otter when a wild duck rose. I shot and killed it, and on picking it up found it had no bill. I thought it unlikely that I had knocked off its bill, and, in returning, dropped in at a farmhouse to have a drink. The farmer inquired what I had shot at.

"A wild duck," I replied, "but it has no bill."

"Ah!" he said, "I can explain that. I tilled a gin out in the gutter last night. The duck was caught by the bill, and, after fluttering, left the bill behind."

He fetched the bill, stuck it on to my duck, and it matched exactly.

One day Major Warry shot at a pheasant which flew right through the dining-room window. We went in and caught the bird, which was not hit, and, having marked it, let it go. We killed the same bird the season after.

When I was at Newton Abbot, a gentleman of the place shot a pheasant above the bedroom window of a cottage. The bird was going at such a speed that it knocked a hole clean through the lath and plaster, and dropped dead.

When I was on Dartmoor, I had a trapper. Going out trapping in a field, we dug up "scrapes" to catch rabbits—*i.e.* made little holes and placed gins in them. Rabbits will always run to good earth. Next morning, instead of rabbits, we found two foxes. We put them in two different bags, and I told the trapper, whose father was a miller and kept a horse, to ride away down to old Fes (tus) Harris, head-keeper to Lady Carew of Haccombe. The old man had often asked me for foxes, which he consigned to a drain. When the hunters came round he would let one of the foxes out, and get a tip. He had nearly always a fox in limbo, and that he might not starve, threw in carrion and rabbits. Not a bad dodge!

I caution keepers against laying eggs on the ground, in order to tempt vermin into traps. Instead of doing so they should fasten a bind round a tree, five or six feet up, and inserting a couple of sticks, make a platform. On this platform they should place both eggs and trap. There will then be no fear of game being caught in the traps.

I CONTINUE KEEPERING

On the hills at Honiton I placed at one time high fir-posts surmounted by round gins, known as hawk-traps, in which were caught hawks, cuckoos, and owls, both brown and white. White owls do no harm, if brown do, and I was always sorry when the former were taken.

I once knew a kestrel hawk's nest, which I let alone until the mother bird began to sit. I then killed the old ones, both male and female, whereupon there came a hen sparrow-hawk and hatched the eggs. As soon as she had hatched them, I killed her, so that I know what I am stating to be a fact.

This was certainly a very extraordinary occurrence, unlike anything that I have ever seen myself or heard mentioned, for the birds belonged to entirely different tribes. To add to my list of wonders, I have caught a hare on Brendon Hill, weighing eleven pounds. On Lady Egremont's property at Orchard Wyndham, I have killed a pheasant weighing five pounds, and, at another time and place, a woodcock weighing eighteen ounces. I have also caught thirty-one rabbits in thirty wires.

As to wiring—a great deal of this is done in the country, ostensibly for taking rabbits. I, for instance, might rent a farm of rabbits, or perhaps a farmer might offer so much for the rabbits, say, twopence a head. Now these men will deny they take anything but rabbits, but I say they do. I've caught dogs, I've caught foxes, I've caught cats—not to mention hares, pheasants, squirrels, rats, and hedgehogs. It is rare to catch a rat, a squirrel, a partridge, or a hedgehog, because they go through the wires. It is possible for them to go through ten times, and never get entangled once. With other creatures it is different. They pull up the wire with their legs, and are caught.

I hear that Mr Sanders is going to give up the stag-hounds. Now suppose the land-owners were to grant me leave to shoot the deer, as I can no longer do so myself, I should pick out a good shot, a farmer's son, and he should not kill twelve stags a year, or one a month. Why do I pitch on a farmer? Because I always found them good shots, whether at flax or feather. I reckoned myself a *fair* shot. I could generally bet as to fifteen shots out of twenty, let the game be running, flying, jumping, or sitting. But it took me all my time to keep up with them. When I was in Devonshire, I had more trouble with farmers than with poachers, because a farmer is never trespassing,

222

whereas, with a poacher, if I saw one out of his path, I could have him up. To see a farmer walking about his yard, you would think that he wouldn't tread on a worm, but those Devonshire farmers, I found, needed to be watched like other folks. When I have been to market, for instance, and returned home, I have been told by people that they have heard shots fired. My advice to keepers, therefore, is to stay at home and go to bed rather than to market; then, it will not be known whether they are in or out. But be sure to keep on good terms with your wife; otherwise, if anyone comes and asks for you, she may let the cat out of the bag, saying that you are lazy or something of the sort. If I wanted to go to bed and had a few "tips" hidden away, I would fetch half-a-sovereign, and, giving it to the old woman, tell her that I wished to lie down a bit. In that case she would reply, "'Twill do ee good to go to bed and rest theeself, and I'll bring ee a cup o' tay byme-by." Women are very fond of money.

Talking of farmers, however, when I was a young man and poached, if I shot on a farm, and the farmer chanced to hear it, he never failed to rush to the stable, jump on his horse, and ride off to the spot where he heard the shot fired. By the time he came up, I was on the opposite side of the hedge, whence I could see the old fellow staring and looking about, his horse with no bridle or saddle on, only an old hempen halter. Now what do you think made him act so? Was it for the landlord's good? Not a bit of it. He did it because I was killing what he considered he ought to have. It was self.

Here are a couple of incidents that will interest gunners. I was out with another man pheasant shooting in King's Brompton parish, when I saw two birds on one tree. I went round to see if I could get both in a line, but found I could not. I therefore arranged with my mate that he should have his gun ready, and that I should plant my foot on the top of his, the understanding being that, when I moved my foot, he was to pull the trigger, and so was I. Well, we happened to pull together, and killed the two birds. It is unnecessary to point out that if we had shot one bird, the other would have flown away.

Another time I was out, and, near New Bridge, saw a pheasant on a tree. Something had happened to my own gun—I believe I had blown out the nipple—so I went home and borrowed an old flint-lock. As the bird was close to the road, I asked a man to accompany me and keep his eye open whilst I shot at it. I loaded the flint-lock gun, and my friend and I hurried to the spot, to find the pheasant still there. I pulled back the old flint-lock cock (or dog), and had a drive, as I thought, at the bird, but the gun didn't go off. Accordingly, I fresh primed it, taking out the old powder and putting new in the pan. Once more I pulled the trigger—"snick" it went again, but again there was no sign of a spark. Evidently the flint was bad. Had a third go; still no use. Then I turned to my mate, and said :

"Shan't give up yet. I shall take out the powder, prime lusty, and whilst I hold the gun to my shoulder, tight, firm and steady, you are to strike the match and apply it."

"All right!" he answered.

It was a funny sensation, as I did not know exactly when the gun was going off. However, it did go off, and down came the old pheasant —wallop! When I reflect on what I accomplished with weapons of that description, I say to myself, "What might I not have done with the guns that are about now?"

CHAPTER IX

IN WHICH I RECOUNT MY EXPERIENCES
AS WATER-BAILIFF

I HAVE now come to the last stage of my
career, but in order to show how I qualified
myself for holding the post of water-bailiff—
I can say without fear it was never held by
a better—I must hark back somewhat to what
may be called the beginning of times; that
is, to the period preceding the regulations that
now obtain, conservators, watchers, licences, and
all the rest. In other words, I will try to give
you a little idea of Barle river as it was fifty
years ago.

On one occasion Sir Thomas Acland
employed us fishermen of Dulverton to draw
the pools on his water. Trammels in those
days were about 16 ft. long, and were sewn
together according to the width of the pool.
A long line was passed through the shackles
at the top of the net, and we drew to the
bottom of the pool, where another net had
been erected. Two dragged the net, one on

each side, and two walked behind to unhitch the net in case it caught in a stick or stone. When we reached the lower net, the object of which was, of course, to prevent the fish going down-stream, both nets were taken out and drawn to land. Well, we went to Sherdon Hutch, on the edge of the Forest, and began to draw. We continued fishing as far as to Bradley Ham, where dinner was waiting for us. Nearly three hundredweight of fish was taken that day, and many gentlemen of Dulverton and the neighbourhood came out to witness the sport. A remarkable thing happened just above Withypool Bridge. So heavy were the nets that Withypool men had to be called in to help them out to land with us. Our dinner had been brought by Mr Paull, of Winsford, in a trap. When we had finished dining, the fish was thrown, like a load of herrings all loose, into the trap, taken round, and given to Sir Thomas's tenantry. Sir Thomas also paid us fishermen for our day's work.

This will show what fish there were in the river then. Many a night I would go out with a trammel, and catch twenty or thirty pounds. At that time fish was threepence or fourpence a pound ; now it is ninepence. How can the scarcity of fish nowadays be accounted for? I know that one, two, three, four, five, six, seven trammels were out every night at Dulverton, leave alone Withypool and Hawk-ridge. It used to be said that the more fish there were caught, the "plentier" they were. There are now four or five bailiffs about, and fish are scarcer than ever. In my opinion the present race of fishermen are degenerate and inefficient. They catch practically nothing. Why, in the old days, Ned Ball, a mason and a fly-fisher, killed from eighteen to twenty pounds a day, and Parson Gould, the principal fisherman of those that visited here, would kill thirty pounds a day. Tom Quick, a man of Dulverton, has carried his fish for him scores of times.

Besides Sir Thomas Acland, old Mr Warren, a miller, who claimed the right to the weir at Dulverton, employed us to draw for him once or twice a year. We generally caught forty or fifty pounds' weight; and he had one half of the fish, and we the other. Rocky Pool and Highleigh Weir belonged to different owners, but as they adjoined, we were hired by the parties in common, and out of these pools we have taken more than a hundred-weight. It is worthy of note that the farther you go down-stream, the bigger the fish.

Once upon a time my love of fish and fishing brought me into trouble. I was strolling up the Dulverton bottom, just to see what was knocking about, and as I could observe nothing, and it was rather hot, thought I would go into the river and tickle a few fish. By-and-by a man came riding along on a horse. It was one of Lord Carnarvon's tenants.

"Well," he said, "what sort of sport have you had?"

"Middling," I replied, never dreaming he would tell of it. (In those days not much notice was taken of fishing.) However, it was not long before my friend Mr Bisset was apprised of the occurrence, and not long before I was summoned for unlawfully fishing. I appeared before the magistrates, who gave me the choice of a fine or a month's imprisonment. I preferred going to jail, as I had by then got used to the place, and had no occasion to fear the treadmill.

On being appointed water-bailiff, I was sent to Simonsbath on the moor. Salmon were very plentiful that year, and my instructions

were to proceed down the river, and see how
many I could count. On returning to Withypool I wanted some refreshment, and entered
the inn for that purpose. On coming out I
found, just outside the door, a salmon stuck
on a pole.

This, no doubt, was done to annoy me. A
hint was given me as to the parties, and I
thought to myself, "I'll be upsides with them."
Accordingly, the following week I went into
a wood close by the river, and watched. About
dinner-time I saw some chaps coming up
along the bank, and they kept looking into
the water.

At last they stopped. One of them went
to the hedge, cut out a stick, fixed a spear
on the end of it, speared a fish with it, and
threw it out on the bank. I was a good way
off, but I bolted after them. They soon saw
me, and ran at the top of their speed towards
the farm from which they had come. There
were three of them—a farmer and two labourers.
I made for the farm, but, though I searched
all the linhays, not a trace of them could I
find. The missus declared she knew nothing
about them. However, I had recognised them
plainly enough, and applied for a summons

against them.   They appeared before the
magistrates — just like myself so many years
before — and, by appealing to Mr Bayly
Collyns, one of the conservators, got off with
a fine of one pound and expenses.

After a while I began to suspect that salmon
were being taken out at Perry water.   I was
up in Pezzlecombe wood, watching, when I
saw a man go down towards the gutters.
There he looked about, and at last he observed
a salmon.   Although I was half-a-mile off, I
had no difficulty in making out his manœuvres,
as Mr Jericho, one of the conservators, had lent
me a pair of field-glasses.   Mr Jericho, I may
mention, was a parson who officiated at Marsh
Chapel and lived at " The Villa," where Mr
Moore does now.   Being a Dulverton man,
he was naturally more disposed to oblige.

Since it was a clear case of poaching, down
I ran across the wood, and, hiding away,
waited till the man should come up.   As he
approached a house, one of the Perry cottages,
he shook up his pocket, as much as to say,
" I've got him."

" Yes, Jack," I cried, jumping out from behind
a pig's loose, " I know all about that.   I know
you've got him."

So saying, I drew near to take away the fish, whereupon he held up the pick.

"Attempt to touch my pocket," he said, "and I'll stab you."

Well, I thought it was not worth while to be stabbed for the sake of a salmon, and I was certain he had caught the fish. I therefore contented myself with answering:

"All right, Jack; you'll be summoned for this."

So he was, and had to pay one pound and costs.

One day a letter arrived from Mr Ford, clerk of the Board, ordering me to Culmstock, a village quite out of our neighbourhood, and ten miles beyond Tiverton. I went to Culmstock, where I met a gentleman fishing without a licence. I stopped him.

"What do you mean?" he said. "You have no authority."

"Here is my warrant," I replied, showing it to him.

"Pooh!" he exclaimed, "that warrant isn't worth a farthing."

However, he found out his mistake. A few days later he was had up at Collumpton, and, though he brought down a barrister from London, was fined a pound.

In the evening I went about the village

232

EXPERIENCES AS WATER-BAILIFF

trying to get lodgings. It happened to be the time when Jack the Ripper was making himself famous, and though I had no connection with that hero, the report of his proceedings stood in my light. I called at two or three public-houses, then at private houses, and finally at the policeman's house. It was no use. His wife replied that he wasn't at home. I met an old fellow, a cripple, who, it seemed, had just come out of the public. I inquired whether he was going home.

"Yes," he replied.

"Can you lodge me?" I asked.

"No," he said.

"Will you let me sit up on a chair or anything?" I asked again. "That would do for me."

"No," he said.

It was all No! They were all afraid of Jack the Ripper. This being so, I thought I would find a lodging for myself, and got into an old linhay, where I stayed till daylight. On coming out, I saw a chimney smoking, and, going to the cottage, begged a cup of tea. I offered to pay the man for it, but, a very good sort of chap, he refused to take anything. Glad, perhaps, to get rid of me.

233

AUTOBIOGRAPHY OF A POACHER

On another occasion, I was sent to Topsham on a Sunday. Between 12 P.M. on Saturday and 6 A.M. on Monday are close hours, during which no one has a right to catch salmon in boats; and my errand was precisely to check any such proceedings. Orders were given me to charter two men, rough fellows, to act as my companions. These I picked up in a public - house at Exeter. They were sturdy chaps, not very old, and by a singular chance each of them had lost an eye in fighting. Down we went to Turf, where the double locks are, and there is a house with a verandah outside, from which Topsham can be seen on the other side of the river. Turf, I suppose everybody knows, is a famous place for white-bait.

After a time a boat came out and crossed to our side. Then a seine, or what you call it—I have little acquaintance with sea-fishing —was thrown out, and the boatmen began to drag it. The moment they stopped dragging and took to hauling in the nets, we slipped across and got down under the banks. Before we could catch them, however, we had to run to the beach, across the open. This was their opportunity. They saw us running, and we arrived just in time, as the saying is, to be too late. They had thrown in their nets, and were on the point of putting off.

Meanwhile, the behaviour of my allies, the two Exeter fellows, perplexed me not a little. They lingered behind, and made no headway at all towards catching the beggars. Indeed, it almost appeared as though the two parties were acting in concert. Just as the boat put off, my companions made a show of swimming out, but the men in the boat got up their oars and swore they would brain the first that attempted to board them. That was quite enough, the Exonians turned tail, and the poachers, having escaped, made fun of us. All this seemed like collusion. On the other hand, one of the Exeter men declared he had seen salmon in the bottom of the boat, and stuck to the assertion, although I never saw any. This, again, was very funny; I could not make the fellows out. It seemed to me that all they were anxious for was to get drinks out of me, and I hope they were satisfied.

After all, they were of some use. They knew the names of the culprits, who were summoned, and, having appeared at Exeter Castle, were each fined three pounds and costs.

AUTOBIOGRAPHY OF A POACHER

One day I was going up beside the river
Barle, when I saw a gentleman fishing. I
noticed from time to time he took something
out, and put it in his pocket. I watched him;
he did it again. I was on the right bank of
the river, and he on the other, so that I could
not see very plainly; but, however, I thought
all was not right. He got out at Newgate,
and went down by the hams, not seeing me.
I walked up to him.

"What sort of sport?" I asked.

"Very poor," he replied. So saying, he
opened his basket and let me see—four or
five trout.

"What about those you have in your pocket?"
I said, and putting my hand into his left pocket,
I drew out several young salmon.

"H'm!" he said, "you are not going to
say anything about it, are you, Holcombe?"
I knew him well, and had often drunk out of
his flask, but, of course, I could not allow such a
circumstance as that to prevent me from doing
my duty. He then offered me money.

"No," I answered, "I take no money."

In the evening a certain gentleman came
to me with half-a-sovereign. That also I
refused. Proper poacher; proper watcher.

EXPERIENCES AS WATER-BAILIFF

I sent an account of the matter to Mr Ford, and took out a summons. Nobody, however, appeared at the justices' meeting. In fact, the summons could not be served, because the culprit, who had been staying at one of the hotels, could not be found. The case was accordingly adjourned, and adjourned it remained for upwards of six months, when the fox was run to earth. The erring gentleman sent a London lawyer to plead for him, but as well have sent a child. He was found guilty, and fined pretty stiff. Altogether, the affair must have cost him pounds.

For reasons to which I need not refer I came to suspect that fish were being taken out of the Exe at Barlynch. Up I went into Execleave, where I could see the meadow and look right down on anything that might happen. Soon I saw an old man come down turning water. After he had been at work a bit, he went down along, and looked into the gutter. Then he dapped the salmon or something— for certain, it was a salmon—with a pick, and threw it out on the grass. There he let it stay for half - an - hour, whilst he continued guttering or turning water. You must know that salmon, in descending a stream, avoid the weirs, not liking to be knocked about, and come down by the gutters or little waters used to irrigate the fields.

When the farmer took up the salmon to carry it away I holloa'd across to him, asking him to put it down until I arrived. He was very good-natured, and did as I requested, although I had to cross the stream by a clammer higher up, and that occupied me a quarter of an hour. I questioned him about the fish, when he replied that he was going to throw it away, give it to the pigs, or something to that effect. I took possession of the salmon, and brought it home. As usual, I communicated with Mr Ford, a summons followed, and the farmer was fined one pound and costs.

It was during the time I was river-watcher that the murder of Archibald Reed took place. Reed was what, I suppose, would be called a colleague of mine, and one morning he was found with his throat gashed, in a place called the Rag, at Tiverton. The terrible affair caused a great sensation throughout the country, and though several persons must have been implicated in the crime, and more than one individual was an object of suspicion, no arrests were made, and to this day the deed is shrouded in mystery. However, when Reed was killed, I was sent for to take his place and remained at Tiverton for several weeks, watching the Exe in company with a policeman. I was not particularly alarmed, but I took the precaution of bringing my pistol with me, and I fancy it would have gone hard with the murderers if they had tried to serve me as they did Reed.

Towards the close of my term as water-bailiff I suffered a great loss by the death of my wife. If my mother had petted me, my wife and mother-in-law indulged me still more. They were always thinking and talking of "their Jack," and studied my comfort in a hundred little ways, of which I was not perhaps entirely deserving. For one thing, and a very important thing, my wife was an extremely clever manager, so that, with all my extravagance, I was able to live well and dress well. The rather extensive wardrobe, which I have saved out of the wreck of my former prosperity, is a monument of her thrift and affection. I believe I have never mentioned an article of apparel by which I set great store. It was a white flowered waistcoat, with threepenny-bits for buttons, and, when sported at our club-walk and on other high days

and holidays, was the envy of the neighbourhood.

On the decease of my beloved partner, I had
once more to shift for myself, and it appeared to
me that my best course was to advertise for
a housekeeper. To this intent I repaired to
Tom Galloway, a shoemaker, and invoked his
help. Tom used to do everybody's writing,
and, as we had been brought up together and
were neighbours, he would have done anything
for me. We drew up an advertisement:—
"Wanted a Housekeeper. Apply Mr John
Holcombe, Dulverton, Somerset," and sent it
to the *Tiverton Gazette*. Meanwhile, as my
house was locked up, the postmaster was requested to leave any letters addressed to me
at Galloway's. A day or two after the notice
was out Tom brought up to Battleton, where I
was lodging, a large parcel of replies, and
throwing it on the table, remarked :

"Here, you've got something to look over.
You'll want a clerk to answer 'em all."

"There won't be many of 'em answered by
me," I replied.

As a matter of fact, out of about fifty letters
I answered, I think, three. On the following
day one of the applicants came from Taunton.

I went to the station to meet her, and she proved to be a fine upstanding young woman, light-haired and fair-complexioned. I saw at a glance that she would not do for me, but, dressed as she was all in her silks, I was not sorry to take her up to Dulverton and cut a dash. It is two miles from Dulverton Station to the town, and as we walked on, I asked her what she could do.

"I have never been used to hard work," was her reply, "not even so much as to wash cups and saucers."

"Then what have you been about all your time?" I queried.

"I've been in Glasgow," she answered, "in a large shop—a showroom."

"Well, you're pretty showy, at any rate," I thought to myself.

On reaching Dulverton I showed her the house, and, as I had a splendid lot of things, she seemed well pleased. After that she knocked about with me all day. When the time came for her to go away, I kept her about on the road, gaming with her, and she lost her train. This was a bit of roguery on my part. It was the last train, and she had to return to Dulverton for the night. When she realised the state of affairs, she was in a fine way.

"I don't know what mother will say!" she cried.

However, I did my best to console her by telling her that I would find her accommodation; and I was as good as my word, for I escorted her to the "Red Lion," a most respectable hotel, and got her a bed. The next morning, after breakfast, I introduced her to my landlady at Battleton, and accompanied her to Mount Sydenham, and other spots, to view the lovely scenery. By this time we were on kissing terms, and I have no doubt she thought I might marry her. Otherwise she was perfectly modest, and didn't care for the public-house.

In the course of the evening, we again set off for the station. I had my watch with me, but I altered it, and caused her once more to lose the train. She telegraphed from the station to her mother, and then returned with me towards Dulverton. As the charges at the "Red Lion" were too high for my pocket, I spoke to the woman at my lodgings, and induced her to give her a bed. The following morning she rose and had breakfast, and, because she wouldn't be licked, went into the town, and bought a time-table. She left by the mid-day train.

Notwithstanding the tricks I had played on her, we parted good friends, and she begged me to meet her at Milverton sometimes, that town being about half-way between Dulverton and Taunton. (Curiously enough, her name was Taunton.) I promised her I would, and a fortnight later took train and found her waiting for me on the railway platform. We stayed about Milverton all day until my train came away at night, when I wished her well. Not long afterwards my sister saw her in a hospital at Taunton. Before this, however, I had called on her at her mother's, and left a present of fish, for which I had been obliged to pay. She in return, sent me a beautiful silk handkerchief. The girl had been well brought up, and I liked her, but she did not suit me. Apart from that, she was twenty-five, and I fifty.

Another candidate came from Taunton, this one of her own accord, and began inquiring where Mr Holcombe lived, evidently with the thought that I was a grand man, and had a fortune. Somebody told me of this, so I went out to meet the woman.

243

"Are you the gentleman that wants a house-keeper?" she asked.

"I ain't a gentleman," I replied, "but I want a housekeeper."

"Oh, well," she said, "I should like to see your house."

So I took her over and unlocked the door. I was not so favourably impressed with her as I was with Miss Taunton. She was about thirty-five, and more of an old farmering woman. After she had looked over the house, she inquired what wages I was disposed to give.

"Haven't made up my mind," I replied.

"Oh," she said, "but you must make up your mind, if you really want a housekeeper."

"I don't know whether you drink or no?" I queried.

"Yes," she answered, "I ain't a teetotaller."

"Well," said I, "I don't keep anything in the house. Perhaps you wouldn't mind stepping over to the 'Lamb.'"

"Not in the slightest," she replied.

We made our way over to the "Lamb," and I asked her what she was going to have.

"A pint o' cider, please, sir."

The cider was drawn, and I think I had a glass of beer. The old woman soon finished her pint, and I then asked if she would take another.

"Yes."

She drank it up appreciatively, while Mrs Tarr, the landlady, and I winked at each other. The sight of the woman was enough —I certainly did not mean to engage her— but I thought it would be unkind to send her away empty. So there she sat and consumed six pints of cider. I began to feel alarmed.

"If you can drink cider like that, and I beer," said I to myself, "the sooner I can get you to the station the better."

So, as soon as I could manage it, we returned to the house, and from there I hurried her down to the station.

Some time elapsed, and I had ceased to expect any more letters, when one morning Galloway tapped at the window, saying :

"Here's a big letter come for you."

I broke open the letter and found it contained a photo from a lady in London, who inquired whether I should like to engage the original. I looked over the likeness, which was that of a funny-looking creature with a Piccadilly fringe, but I could see that she was out of the common. The letter desired me to forward my likeness in return, and in the evening I sent it off. Very soon another letter arrived, in which the lady was good enough to say that she liked my features, and asked me to state if I was fond of music. I replied that I was—very.

The next letter from the lady—a proper lady, I believe — was rather pointed. She wanted to know what yearly income I was possessed of. On reading that, I caused a reply to be sent to the effect that my income came out of the sinking fund. This finished the business. She wrote to me once more to say that "ma" and "da" had told her to give up all correspondence. I received the announcement calmly, as I considered that, if Jack did not suit "ma" and "da," neither would "ma" and "da" suit Jack. I forgot to say that she returned my photo, and I, of course, returned hers.

There is little more to add. The whole business was somewhat foolish—at any rate, as we conducted it ; so, having looked over the old letters, I burnt them in a bundle.

CHAPTER X

HOW I FINISHED UP

I SERVED the conservators for fifteen whole years — and then I got the sack. Strange as it may seem, I have not even to this day the slightest inkling of the cause. All I know is that, one day in his office, the late Mr Ford remarked,

"I think, Holcombe, it would be better to have a change."

As I was quite content with my place, and looking forward to a pension, I rather demurred to this, and replied,

"I don't know, sir, about that."

However, Mr Ford repeated, "It would be better to have a change," and soon after I received a formal notice terminating the engagement. At the time this decision seemed most mysterious, and I could find no more likely reason for it than my good behaviour. Since then I have pondered the matter, and am inclined to attribute my dismissal to politics or malice — perhaps both. I recollect

247

that not long before I was sent about my business, I had visited the river Culm, where I had found three hutches. These hutches were on the estate of a gentleman well known as a Liberal. On reaching Tiverton, I saw one of the conservators, who was a Conservative in politics, and mentioned what I had seen.

Now Mr Ford was a rank Liberal, and I have sometimes thought that the fact of my speaking to the Conservative gentleman before reporting the matter to him, may have prejudiced him against me. As for my own politics, I make no concealment of them. Both on public and private grounds I am a Conservative. I have had Conservative, and I have had Liberal masters, and I much prefer the former. Liberals are hollow, and turn like a weathercock. Besides, if what I read in the papers is correct, Liberals care nothing for Old England, and would sell the country for a trifle. No doubt my opinions, the opinions of an old poacher, will not influence the public, but I wish to speak as I find, and that is my experience.

Perhaps, however, it was not all politics. Very likely some kind neighbour may have hinted to the conservators that I neglected my

work and spent too much time in the public-
houses. Of course, I don't for a moment admit
the accusation ; at the same time, I am free to
say that, in my view, it would be a good thing
if the present regulations were abolished and the
watchers paid for staying at home in bed. How
was it in the old days? The stones used to be
loose, giving the trout a harbour. We put a
net over them, moved the stones with a bar of
iron, and out popped a fish. The eels, too, that
I have seen eating up the trout's spawn like a
dog eating whit-pot, were killed in large numbers,
and the fish had a better chance of getting away
from the otters. "The more trout you catch,
the more plentiful they are," I have said, and
truly, for you catch the big ones that eat the
small ones like fun.

After my dismissal, a man called Marwood
was sent to Dulverton, and, meeting me, he said :

"Here, I have been told to come to you, as
you have been river-watcher, and get a wrinkle
or two from you."

"Oh, all right!" I replied. "You can come
and lodge with me if you like." And so he did,
he and his wife and two children. The result of
this arrangement was that I knew all his doings
by night and day ; and whether he was up, and

where he went to. The information thus gained I conveyed to the Dulverton poachers, and they never in their lives had such a successful season. Marwood had a namesake, a hangman; and after he left me, he went to live in a court off High Street, known thenceforth as " Hangman's Alley." He was very unpopular, and at last nearly bummed out of the place.

I did not take my dismissal tamely. Instead of granting me a proper pension they gave me what I believe they called a " solatium," or some Greek word. This was merely five shillings a week for twenty weeks, and I considered it entirely insufficient. I thought I would do something, therefore, to be even with them, bought a new trammel at Southmolton, and with this paid them home by littles. Altogether I killed four hundredweight of fish, six of them twelve and a half pounds. But I had been hit hard. I got a little work in and out—binding wood, digging potatoes, gardening, and the like —but found I could not earn enough to live and keep house. Without saying a word to anybody I left my (second) wife and went into the work-house. That I did not like at all. Of the two, I would rather go to prison. It is possible that, as the infirmities of age increase, I may have to return, but I earnestly hope not. For one thing, there is no tea.

After three or four days' stay, I came out of the workhouse, and went on as before, doing odd jobs, and lodging with my brother-in-law at the Rock. But again I found I could not earn sufficient to keep myself properly. A dreadful thought now entered my head. I took three ropes, and went up into Mr Tarr's linhay. Tying one end of a rope to the beam, I put the other round my neck, and hanged myself. Some boy stood by and looked at me, and, before it was too late, ran out and told Mr German, who cut the rope. Having done that, he escorted me back to the Rock, and sent for the bobby. The bobby arrived shortly after, and conveyed me to lock-up. The next morning I had a visitor—Mr Sydenham, the doctor.

" What have you been about, John ? " he asked. " Trying to hang yourself, haven't you ? "

" Yes," I said.

" And do you mean to do it again?" he inquired.

" I ain't particular about myself," I replied.

Then another visitor appeared—Mr Mildmay, the magistrate. He put several questions to me, and requested me to state whether I would go to quarter sessions or to the Wells Asylum.

"If you will be advised by me," he said, "you will go to the asylum, where you will be better cared for than in prison."

I assented, and was removed accordingly. On entering the establishment, I was brought before the doctor, and had the same sort of conversation with him as with the Dulverton physician.

"Did you hang yourself?"

"Yes."

"Going to do it again?"

"Well, no," I replied, "the rope galled."

"Ah!" he said, "I see what is the matter with you—the Devil and the drink." In which, no doubt, he was right.

I remained at the asylum for some little time, and got on capitally. The doctors saw there was nothing wrong with me, and I was set to look after the "lunies." So far as I was concerned, I did not object. I regarded the whole thing as a spree, and thought I had got into a nice crib. But I could not help feeling sorry for the unhappy inmates. Some of them would strip stark naked, some would fight, and some would drop on their knees, praying. Poor fellows!

A young doctor used to say to me,

"You know you'll have to stay here a considerable time—perhaps twelve months."

HOW I FINISHED UP

The old doctor knew better. In six weeks I was out, and returned home all right. In one sense the change did me a lot of good. We had plenty of meat, and plenty of tea and coffee, but no beer. This led me to reflect. If I did not drink inside the asylum, why need I drink outside? On the staff was a man named Monday, who had been in the Dulverton police, and who now enlightened me in religious matters. With regard to drinking he told me the last thing he did with his barrel of beer was to take it outside the door, and let the beer run out. The upshot is, that I have not drunk a drop since. I must not forget to mention that I learnt warding so well that I was employed to accompany a man not exactly right from Dulverton to London, look after him whilst there, and bring him back, if possible, safe and sound. The errand was a complete success.

My tale is told. Like most men past seventy, I live a very humdrum life, though more industrious than ever before. In the words of the song,

> "I am growing old, and my locks are gray,
> No more shall I dance with the young and the gay,
> For time has determined the truth to unfold,
> I've a mark in my forehead to show I am old."

AUTOBIOGRAPHY OF A POACHER

I attend church in the morning, and the Lower Chapel, where I take sacrament, in the evening. I also read the Bible. "And, I hope you are penitent?" I fancy I hear somebody say. Penitent about what? Not about poaching, for I can't find a word in the Bible against it. I have not caused this book to be written as an encouragement to youngsters, and I should think very few, if any, would choose to face such hardships as I have been through, insomuch that it is a miracle I am alive; nevertheless, if you desire a plain statement, I will answer candidly that, if I had my time over again, I should certainly prefer poaching to game-keeping. To see a deer at the head of a wood, to shoot him, to watch him tumble down, nobody can tell what a spree it is! (And there was no fining, remember, in my day.) Or to hear the hares come out into the nets, and cry ten thousand murders! Or to march round the trees and try to kill two pheasants at a shot! These are the pleasures on which my mind feeds now in my old age, and I hope my kind friends, especially the stag-hunters, will forgive me for it. Seeing that the law has made deer-killing impossible, I am disposed to wish them well. They take

HOW I FINISHED UP

out the hounds after Exford and Winsford fairs, and do all they can to provide sport for the foot-people, whom I should be delighted to join, if I were not so old and partially dependent on "Tom Parish." But you see how it is—I must make hay while the sun shines. That reminds me. A man I met out harvesting the other day had heard it said up at London that the old deer-killer, Lord Mansfield, must be dead, because deer were so plentiful. No, I am not dead, but just a little past my ancient agility. That, however, shall not prevent my proposing the toast — (Peace to you, Dr Collyns!)—SUCCESS TO STAG-HUNTING!

255